The Utterly, Completely, and Totally Useless
Fact-O-Pedia

The Utterly, Completely, and Totally Useless

Fact-O-Pedia

A Startling Collection of Over 1000 Things
You'll *Never* Need to Know!

Charlotte Lowe

HarperCollins*Publishers*

HarperCollins*Publishers*
77–85 Fulham Palace Road,
Hammersmith, London W6 8JB

www.harpercollins.co.uk

Published by HarperCollins*Publishers* 2009

1 3 5 7 9 10 8 6 4 2

Charlotte Lowe asserts the moral right to
be identified as the author of this work

Interior illustrations by Gary Bennett

A CIP catalogue record for this book is
available from the British Library

ISBN: 978-0-00-783793-9

Printed and bound in China by
South China Printing Co. Ltd

This book is dedicated to my mom,
for her tireless encouragement and her inimitable spirit for life.

Acknowledgments

I'd like to thank my friends and family for all their contributions, opinions, and patience. I'd also like to extend my gratitude to Shannon Kerner for her valuable support. Above all, thank you to my editor Jeannine Dillon, who provided relentless commitment around the clock to both me and this project.

Contents

Introduction

"I love talking about nothing. It is the only thing I know anything about."
—Oscar Wilde

I started my career in New York where days were spent at work and evenings were devoted to some form of social gathering whether it was a dinner, a cocktail night, an art opening, etc. Being in my 20s at the time—hopeful, ambitious and brimming with drive to climb to the top—I was exercising the freedoms and liberties of youth, and exploiting the opportunities to meet and interact with new people.

With a different event every night, introductions were common and frequent. At first, they always seemed awkward but eventually, like with any skill, a little practice goes a long way. It became quite easy to meet people, particularly in New York, because no matter where you are or whom you are with, the same questions always get asked. You can even time them! By the third sip of the first drink, the inevitable roster begins: *Where are you from? Where do you live? What do you do?*

The first two questions don't really require much thought. *I'm from Toronto. I am currently living in an apartment that can only be the equivalent of a corrugated cardboard shoebox.* However, asking what a person does is a different story altogether. This third question seems the most ambiguous and unclear because it could refer to a number of things, though career is the common answer. *Y-A-W-N*. How is a job the most relevant aspect of our being? Is the question quantified by time or by level of interest? After all, a passion or hobby is every bit as valuable as a full-time job and can provide as much, if not more, gratification. I certainly enjoy my work, but I garner much more fulfillment from my various other pastimes. That said, the next time I am asked that dreaded third question, I will not be an editor or a writer. Nope. I will tell people that I am a Philomath.

Yes, a Philomath! Unbeknownst to me when I first learned the word, a Philomath is *not* a type of pastry equation. It's defined as a person who seeks out knowledge or facts. I am a Philomath, and I receive immense pleasure from it.

I had an avid curiosity for random knowledge over a broad range of subjects from current affairs and the environment to technology and arts. I developed most of my interest while attending school as a young girl: the most obscure facts were often the most compelling. And what I learned, I would share with the most unsuspecting audience: my younger brother, friends, but most often, a pet turtle named Nigo.

Through college and my adult years, I retained that keen interest for learning and discovery, but I found obscure trivia and facts may not work in all circumstances. For example, in a discussion about John F. Kennedy's foreign policies, there may be a split-second window of opportunity to express the former president's love for fish chowder soup. With the right time and delivery, you could be hailed as charming and amusing. The wrong time may also summon a shared group look of confusion and perplexity.

I was ecstatic when presented with the opportunity to write this book. It gave me the chance to aggregate old and new facts and compile them into a tome that would be shared with people and pets beyond my immediate scope. This is a collection accrued through my child- and adult-hood, and I hope that the readers find as much enjoyment in the facts as I did in researching and preparing them.

Are the facts actually useless? Designed to entertain as much as to inform, they do make great start-ups for general conversations and will easily find their way into your daily mix. Just the other day, a friend and I were strolling along the snowy sidewalks of Toronto when he expressed his concerns about proper footwear for the upcoming days. Though the temperature was forecasted to be 0°C, I was able to tell him that the pavement would be salted and the water ice would melt because salt lowers the melting/freezing point of water. I'd conclude that was far from useless!

Anton Chekhov once stated "knowledge is of no value unless you put it into practice." *The Useless Fact-o-pedia* should be shared with others. Sure, cats delivering mail in Belgium or the blue people in a small Kentucky town have limited conversation mileage, but these general facts are sure to draw interest. As well, the relationship between Dolly the cloned sheep and the famed country chanteuse of the same name may seem completely random, but the knowledge is both mirthful and memorable.

Whether you're looking to improve your gift of gab or hone your conversation skills, this book features an A–Z of fascinating factoids. With more than 1000 points, you're sure to win the crowd at any dinner party or social event. Covering everything from absinthe and baseball to Elvis and Spam, you'll discover a cornucopia of riveting facts to keep you engaged time and time again. Enjoy!

Acrobatics

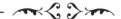

❧ Initially referred only to tightrope walking, acrobatics is a blanket term for nearly any performance or sport which involves full-body activity— especially in short, highly controlled bursts.

❧ Generally, a wire over 20 ft high will be regarded as a high-wire act.

❧ Stephen Peer, a seasoned tightrope walker, died on June 22, 1887 when he fell into Niagara Falls after drinking with some friends.

❧ In China, approximately 100,000 students are currently studying at schools dedicated to the art of acrobatics. High honor is conferred upon those skilled enough to become acrobats because of the unusual and difficult nature of the feats involved.

❧ Seeking a career in the performing arts, Cirque du Soleil founder Guy Laliberté toured Europe as a folk musician and street performer after quitting college. By the time he returned back home to Canada in 1979, he had learned the art of fire breathing and by 1983, the Quebec government granted him 1.5 million Canadian dollars to host the first Cirque du Soleil production.

A

Airplane

~❧ In February 1992, Israeli air force reserve major Ishmael Yitzhaki was convicted of stealing a WWII Mustang fighter plane and flying it to Sweden, where he sold it for $331,000. How did he manage it? He removed the plane from the air force museum by saying it needed painting.

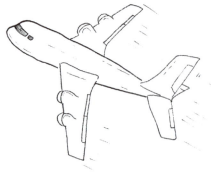

~❧ In a 2008 interview on *The Today Show*, Kareem Abdul-Jabbar revealed that he was once asked on a European flight to sit in the cockpit during takeoff just so the crew could say they flew with his character "Roger Murdoch" from the film, *Airplane*.

A

~❧ A Boeing 747 has six million parts and half of them are fasteners.

~❧ Records indicate that man's first attempt at flying dates back to 1020 when an English monk named Oliver of Malmesbury strapped a pair of wings to his body and attempted to soar the air from Malmesbury Abbey. Consequently, he fell and broke both legs.

~❧ The fastest manned and highest flying aircraft is the North American X-15. It was launched from under the wing of a B-52 and boasts a world speed record 4,520 mph.

Alcohol

🐦 The word alcohol is derived from the Arabic word *al-kuhl*, meaning "finely divided" which is a reference to distillation. It was introduced into the English language around 1543.

🐦 The word "toast" is a wish of good health. It started in ancient Rome, where a piece of toasted bread was dropped into wine.

🐦 Some older terms for hangover include "wailing of cats" (German), "out of tune" (Italian), "woody mouth" (French), "workmen in my head" (Norwegian), and "pain in the roots of my hair" (Swedish).

A

🐦 During Prohibition, temperance activists hired a scholar to delete all references to alcohol beverages from the Bible.

🐦 Since the recent discovery of late Stone Age beer jugs, it's been suggested that fermented beverages existed as early as the Neolithic period (cir. 10,000 BC), and that beer may have preceded bread as a staple.

🐦 Subyou, a powdered alcohol sold in gas stations, convenience stores, and bars across Germany, contains 4.8% alcohol by volume. Marketed as an energy drink, the powder is intended to be mixed with cold water and costs between two to three dollars. Because the product is in powdered form, the manufacturers manage to avoid a tax on it. A similar powdered product was available in the U.S. about 30 years ago and never caught on.

Alice's Adventures in Wonderland

❧ *Alice's Adventures in Wonderland* (1865) had originally been titled *Alice's Adventures Underground.* The original draft was published in 1886.

❧ Author Charles Lutwidge Dodgson used the pen name "Lewis Carroll" when he published the book. The book is reportedly filled with allusions to his friends (and enemies).

❧ Although Tweedledum, Tweedledee, Humpty Dumpty and the Jabberwock are included in film versions called "Alice in Wonderland," these characters did not appear in the original *Alice's Adventures in Wonderland*; but rather, the sequel *Through the Looking-Glass.*

❧ The patient with "Alice in Wonderland Syndrome" suffers from distorted space, time and body image and has feelings and/or visual hallucinations that the entire body or part of it has been altered in shape and size. The majority of patients with the syndrome has a family history of migraine headaches or has overt migraines themselves. Perhaps not coincidentally, Lewis Carroll suffered from severe migraines—also known as a Lilliputian hallucination.

❧ In 1931, the book was banned in Hunan, China, because animals spoke using human language.

A

Alphabet

🖎 "Alphabet" is derived from the first two letters of the Greek alphabet: alpha and beta.

🖎 There were only 23 letters in the Classical Latin alphabet. During medieval times, the letter "I" was used for both "I" and "J," and the letter "V" was used for "U," "V," and "W." Hence the 26 letters in the modern alphabet.

🖎 An *abjad*, also called a consonantary or consonantal alphabet, is a vowel-less alphabet system which still exists in scripts such as Arabic, Hebrew, and Syriac.

A

🖎 The earliest known alphabet was devised in Ugarit in present-day Syria around 1500 BC.

🖎 The Hawaiian Alphabet only contains 12 letters: a, e, i, o, u, h, k, l, m, n, p, and w. Every word ends with a vowel. Where most languages have a larger syllable repertoire, there are only 162 possible syllables in Hawaiian.

Antarctica

❧ Approximately 98% of Antarctica's surface is covered in ice.

❧ In March 2008, researchers discovered giant sea stars or star fish measuring 24 in across during a 35-day census in Antarctic waters.

❧ There is no indigenous population to the continent but the varied seasonal population of researchers is estimated at 1,000.

❧ Bundle up! On average, Antarctica is the coldest, driest, and windiest continent and also boasts the highest average elevation. Since there is little precipitation, except along the coasts, the interior of the continent is technically considered the largest desert in the world.

❧ Early Antarctic explorers actually thought penguins were fish and classified them as such.

A

Arch of Triumph

 The Arch of Triumph (*Arc de Triomphe*) in Paris, France, is more than another tourist attraction drawing millions each year; it's a monument that had been commissioned in 1806 after the victory at Austerlitz by Emperor Napoleon and is inscribed with all of the names of generals and wars fought along the inside and the top of the arch. There are 660 names inscribed on the Arch and underneath is the tomb of an unknown soldier from World War I.

 Napoleon originally planned a statue of a giant elephant in this spot to symbolize his power and the strength of France. We wonder what compelled him to change his mind.

 Visitors can either climb 284 steps to reach the top of the Arch or take the lift and walk up 46 steps. Which is really nothing when compared with the Eiffel Tower which has 1,710 steps or the Empire State Building which has a staggering 1,860. It would do wonders for the gluts.

 A couple of replicas have been created around the world. Bucharest, Romania has an Arch of Triumph to honor the bravery of Romanian soldiers who fought in World War I while the Paris Hotel in Las Vegas has a replica arch which is two-thirds the size of the original.

Aristotle

🐦 "We must not listen to those who urge us to think human thoughts since we are human, and mortal thoughts since we are mortal; rather, we should as far as possible immortalize ourselves and do all we can to live by the finest element in us—for if it is small in bulk, it is far greater than anything else in power and worth."—Aristotle

🐦 Aristotle wrote *Sense and Sensibilia* around 350 BC, about 2159 years before Jane Austen wrote *Sense and Sensibility* (1811)!

🐦 In his treatise "The Politics," he noted that different musical melodies, modes, and rhythms yielded different responses from listeners. He argued that since music has the power of forming character, it should be an important part of the education of the young.

🐦 Aristotle traveled to the island of Lesbos to research the botany and zoology of the island.

🐦 In 2008, the people of Lesbos took a gay group to court to have the group barred from using "lesbian" in its name. As one plaintiff stated, ""My sister can't say she is a Lesbian," said Dimitris Lambrou. "Our geographical designation has been usurped by certain ladies who have no connection whatsoever with Lesbos," he said.

🐦 In Western drama, he created the term "catharsis," the purging of viewers' emotions through pity and fear. He also believed that the action of a play should take place within no more than 24 hours, have one location, and have only one main plot.

A

Backgammon

❧ Some ways of cheating in backgammon include moving the checker the wrong number of spaces; using magnetic, shaved, or weight-loaded dice; using special throws to produce the dice number desired; or having assistance from a third party.

❧ Lars Trabolt from Denmark was the 2008 World Backgammon Champion.

❧ Named after Kit Woolsey—the backgammon expert and former editor of the online backgammon magazine *Gammonline*—the "Woolsey Rule" suggests to double when it is not clear whether a position is a take or a pass.

B

❧ The most expensive backgammon set in the world is Bernard Maquin's design for the Charles Hollander Collection. It boasts 61,082 black, white, and yellow diamonds with a total carat weight of 2071.48. Together with over 6.77 kg of gold, 150 g of silver, and more than 10,000 hours of labor, it retails somewhere between $1.5–2 million. Out of your price range? A mini backgammon set on Ebay sets you back $1.99.

❧ Dream weaving…to see a backgammon game in a dream signifies the presence of an unwelcome guest in the near future. To play a losing game of backgammon represents misfortunes in love, suggesting that the dreamer seeks the wrong type of person and the pursuit for love will be an upward battle.

Bacteria

~ Top of the class…in Florida, a 7th grade student won a school science fair by proving there was more bacteria in ice machines at fast-food restaurants than in toilet bowl water.

~ According to University of Arizona researchers, the TV remote controls in hospital rooms are worse carriers of bacteria than the toilet handles.

~ Kitchen sponges and dish cloths across American homes are prime breeding ground for the most dangerous sources of virulent bacteria, including E. coli, Salmonella, and Staphylococcus. They provide a source of moisture, a ready food supply in the form of food particles, and an easy surface to which the bacteria may cling. They can easily be disinfected however, by placing the sponge in a microwave oven for 60 to 120 seconds. The odor is improved too!

~ Heavy duty…there are approximately five nonillion (5 × 1030) bacteria on Earth, making much of the world's biomass.

~ That could be why sales of hand sanitizers have exploded in the U.S. In 2005, more than $67 million dollars worth of hand sanitizers were sold…a 50% increase from the previous year.

~ "Extreme Barophiles" are bacteria which live at depths greater than 10,000 meters. They are so biologically different from sea level bacteria that they die in a few hours if brought to the surface.

B

Ballet

- Ballet emerged in the late 15th century Renaissance court culture of Italy, as a dance interpretation of fencing. It was eventually further developed in the French court from the time of Louis XIV in the 17th century.

- The word "tutu" may be a corruption of "cucu", French baby talk for "cul-cul" meaning roughly "botty-wotty" (for bottom). Alternatively, it may derive from tulle, the material from which tutus are often made.

- For its first 100 years, ballet was performed exclusively by male courtiers as an amateur entertainment.

- The largest ballet class involved 989 participants in an event organized by Andrew Warth in Canal Walk Shopping Centre, Cape Town, South Africa, on August 24, 2008.

- Just for kicks! A *fouette* is a bit like a pirouette where the dancer flicks their leg around to spin. New Yorker Leigh Zimmerman twirled a new world record by completing 38 complete spins at the Pineapple Dance Studios in London.

- Anna Pavlova, the renowned prima ballerina, died of pneumonia three weeks before her 50th birthday. Following an old ballet tradition, on the day she was to have next performed, the show went on as scheduled, with a single spotlight circling an empty stage where she would have been. The Pavlova dessert—a meringue with fresh fruit and cream—was named after her.

B

Bamboo

❧ Tall order! Bamboo is the fastest-growing woody plant on the Earth, growing as fast as 47.6 in in a 24-hour period.

❧ Many bamboos only flower at intervals as long as 60 or 120 years, and the flowering occurs simultaneously with all plants in the population. Subsequently, the plants produce flowers, which then produce seeds, and then die off. A new crop requires ten years to grow to full maturity.

❧ Newsflash! Some of the world's top inventors found uses for bamboo. Thomas Edison tried over 100 varieties of bamboo for the filament in his first electric bulb, and the only one that worked was the Kyoto bamboo. Also, the needle in Alexander Graham Bell's first phonograph was made of bamboo.

B

❧ Research in China's Qinling Mountains showed giant pandas can consume, on average, 40 pounds of fresh bamboo leaves per day.

❧ The *shakuhachi*, a Japanese end-blown flute, was traditionally made from bamboo. It means "1.8 feet," referring to its size, and was used in classic Japanese music often associated with Zen Buddhism or meditation.

❧ Because the bamboo is made up of more water than normal trees, it releases 35% more oxygen than trees.

Barbie®

- Barbie® was modelled after a German doll named "Lilli" who, in turn, was inspired by a racy, German cartoon strip. The saucy Bild Lilli doll was sold in smoke shops and bars.

- Two Barbie® dolls are sold somewhere in the world every second of every day.

- If Barbie® were a real person her measurements would be an impossible 36–18–38.

- *It's not you, it's me.* On Feb 12, 2004, Mattel announced that Barbie® and Ken had broken up.

- The smash-hit song "Barbie Girl" by Aqua sold eight million copies worldwide and topped many lists including *Rolling Stone*'s "20 Most Annoying Songs" and VH1's "Most Awesomely Bad Songs…Ever." Mattel sued the record label, MCA, and even took the case to the Supreme Court, stating copyright and trademark violation. The case was dismissed.

B

Baseball

❧ The first five members to be inducted into the Baseball Hall of Fame in 1935 were Walter Johnson, Christy Matthewson, Babe Ruth, Honus Wagner, and Ty Cobb.

❧ Baseball evolved in the early 17th century out of a family of English folk games including rounders, stoolball, and cricket.

❧ Still coming to terms with baseball? A swinging strikeout is often called a "whiff" and a batter who is struck out by a fastball is often said to have been "blown away."

❧ Getting to second base is easier than you think. Second is the easiest base to steal, because the catcher must throw a farther distance.

B

❧ In 2008, Alex Rodriguez's salary peaked at $28,000,000, making him the highest-paid baseball player of the year. His career salary at the time was $198,416,252.

❧ The green underside of a baseball cap serves to reduce the light reflection that could distract the ballplayers during daytime games.

❧ An inspector from Major League Baseball visits every ballpark at least twice a year and checks the specifications of the mound including height of the mound, slope of the mound, size of the pitcher's circle; flatness of the pitcher's rubber; and flatness of the area on which the pitcher's rubber is laid.

Bats

❧ One of the rarest mammals in the United States, the spotted bat has the largest ears of any bat species native to North America.

❧ If a bat flies into your home, simply open all the doors and windows and allow it to find its own way out. If this fails to remove the pest, take a large towel or blanket, throw it over the animal, gather it up, and put it outside. The bat should extricate itself from the cloth without any additional handling.

B

❧ The Giant Golden-Crowned Flying Fox has a wingspan of 5 ft and the mammal weighs approximately 3 lbs.

❧ In German, it was once believed that one who donned the left eye of a bat as a talisman would become invisible. Sufficed to say, the trend was short-lived after people were seen fashioning the eyes of dead bats.

❧ The sound of music—white-winged vampire bats, the closest living relative of the common vampire bat, can sing well-coordinated duets with each other.

Beef

~&~ Clara Peller, the elderly actress who first voiced the infamous Wendy's slogan *"Where's the Beef?"*, was later fired after cutting a commercial for spaghetti sauce where she answers her famous question by saying, "I found it."

~&~ Beefaroni contains vitamin A and no other vitamins.

~&~ Selfridges, the renowned London department store, is said to offer the world's most expensive sandwich at £85. The ingredients of the sandwich are: Wagyu beef, fresh lobe foie gras, black truffle mayonnaise, brie de meaux, rocket, red pepper, and mustard confit and English plum tomatoes. You have to pay extra if you want a pack of chips on the side.

~&~ Beefalo, also known as catalo or cattalo, is a hybrid beef animal, bred by crossing the domestic Pulled Angus with the American Bison. Texan Charles Goodnight developed the beefalo in the mid-19th century as he preferred bison meat to beef and, with this hybrid, sought to combine the good flavor of the bison with the Angus's resistance to certain diseases and pests.

~&~ Kobe beef is an exclusive beef from the black Tajima-ushi breed of Wagyu cattle, raised according to strict tradition in Japan. Its distinct flavor, melt-in-your-mouth tenderness, and fatty well-marbled texture is due in large part to the unusual rearing process. Some of it includes feeding beer to the cattle during summer months to stimulate their appetite, massaging the cow to relieve stress and muscle stiffness, and brushing the haircoat with sake to improve the haircoat and softness of skin, which will in turn affect the meat quality.

B

❧ Acclaimed self-taught chef Fergus Henderson of St John restaurant in London has been lauded in Britain, the U.S., and Europe for his "nose-to-tail" style of cooking. The menus at St John offers dishes using the most unusual parts—heart, chitterlings, kidneys, brain, and bone marrow to name a few—to create exceptional dishes. His restaurant is considered one of the world's best.

Bell, Alexander Graham

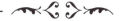

❧ In 1888, Alexander Graham Bell was the president of the National Geographic Society.

❧ His father, grandfather, and brother were all associated with work on elocution and speech, and both his mother and wife were deaf.

❧ Mark Twain expressed initial interested in Bell's company but decided against an investment of $5000, because he saw possibilities in another invention called the Paige typesetting machine. Unfortunately, the machine proved to be much less successful and cost Twain an investment of $250,000. By 1894, Twain declared bankruptcy.

❧ Ring my bell…On March 7, 1876, the U.S. patent office issued a patent on Bell's invention that sent words over a wire by converting the sound waves to a varying current of electricity. This is arguably the single most valuable patent in history.

❧ The film, *The Story of Alexander Graham Bell* debuted in 1939. After it was released, the telephone was commonly called the "Ameche" which was a slang reference to the actor Don Ameche who played the telephone's inventor.

B

Bible

❧ On October 22, 1987 a Japanese buyer, Eiichi Kobayashi, purchased the Old Testament portion of a Gutenberg Bible for $5.4 million at a Christie's Auction. The last sale of a complete version took place nine years before, again at Christie's, for $2.2 million. Today, single pages from first-edition Bibles fetch $25,000 each.

❧ The Tynesdale Bible, translated by William Tyndale, was the first printed Bible in the English language and the New Testament was published in 1526. Before Tyndale completed the second edition, he was taken up and burned for heresy in Flanders.

❧ When ancient scribes copied earlier books, they wrote notes on the margins of the page (marginal glosses) to comment or correct their text—especially if a scribe accidentally omitted a word or line. When later scribes were copying the copy, they were sometimes uncertain if a note was intended to be included as part of the text. Over time, different regions evolved different versions, each with its own assemblage of omissions and additions.

❧ In addition to providing their well-known Bibles in hotel rooms, the Gideons also distribute Bibles to members of the military of various countries, to hospitals, nursing homes, and prisons.

B

Birth

🕊 Lotus Birth is the practice of leaving the umbilical cord uncut after birth so that the baby is left attached to its placenta until the cord naturally separates.

🕊 In 2008, a 70-year-old Indian woman, Omkari Panwar, gave birth to twins, via emergency cesarean section. Omkari became pregnant through IVF treatment so she and her husband could produce a male heir. The babies weighed 2 lbs each.

🕊 The youngest birth was by a five-year-old girl in 1939, by C-section. Her parents, who assumed their daughter had a tumor, took her to a hospital, where she was determined to be seven-months pregnant.

🕊 In 1888, German obstetrician Karl Crede invented the first artificial incubator for premature babies. Because electricity was not widely available, the air inside was warmed by a kerosene lamp.

🕊 According to the U.S. Census Bureau (2007), the world birth rate is at 4.2 births per second.

🕊 On July 22, 1971, Dr. Gennaro Montanino of Rome, Italy, announced he had removed the fetuses of ten girls and five boys from the womb of a 35-year-old housewife during her fourth month of pregnancy. The unborn babies were 5 in long and 5 oz. in weight.

🕊 Heavy duty! Topping the scales at 22 lb 8 oz, the heaviest surviving baby was a boy born to Carmelina Fedele in September 1955 in Aversa, Italy.

B

Black Hole

❧ According to Reinhard Genzel of the Max Planck Institute for Extraterrestrial Physics in Garching, the black hole weighs the equivalent of 4.31 million suns, with an uncertainty of plus or minus 0.36 million. The observations also pinpoint the distance from the Earth to the galaxy's center at 27,000 light-years.

❧ The black hole emits X-ray radiation. The rays get smaller and smaller until they disappear, or "evaporate."

❧ The gravity around the "hole" of a black hole is so strong that nothing can make its way back out after a critical distance. This critical distance at which nothing, not even light, can escape is called the Event Horizon.

❧ "Blackhole Sun" was a song written in 1994 by Chris Cornell of the band Soundgarden. The single has sold over 3 million copies worldwide and can be rocked out on the videogame Rock Band and sung on the games Karaoke Revolution Presents: American Idol Encore and SingStar 90s.

B

Black Widow

🖐 True Black Widow Spiders have the most potent spider venom, which can cause swellings up to 6 in.

🖐 The females can live for up to five years, while a male's lifespan is much shorter. The female, on occasion, eats the male after mating. This form of sexual cannibalism has been observed in the wild only with the southern black widow species.

🖐 The female hangs belly upward and rarely leaves the web.

🖐 Many spiders of the genus *Steatoda* are often mistaken for widow spiders, and are known as false black widows. Their poison can be painful, but not necessarily fatal.

B

🖐 In 2006, Jason Fricker from Dorchester spent three days in a hospital after being bit three times on the chest and stomach when a false black widow fell down the front of his shirt. Although the false black widow has been in Britain since the 1870s (reportedly arriving in bananas from the Canary Islands), its numbers and range have grown in the UK due to milder climates.

🖐 Margaret Rudin made headlines in 1995 as "the black widow" in the shooting death of her fifth husband. The skull and some charred bones of her husband were found in 1995 in a desert about 45 miles from Las Vegas. Prosecutors said she killed him to get a 60 percent share of his $11 million fortune. She was convicted of his murder in 2001.

Blood

 Blood has a long road to travel. There are about 60,000 miles of blood vessels in the human body. And the hard-working heart pumps about 2,000 gallons of blood through those vessels every day.

 An average adult contains five to six quarts of blood in their body.

 Most donated red blood cells can be stored for forty-two days.

 If you begin at age 17 and donate every 56 days until you reach 79 years old, you will have donated 46.5 gallons of blood during that time.

 Most tropical marine fish can survive in a tank filled with human blood.

B

Blue Jeans

🕊 Italian sailors from Genoa, whom the French called Genes, wore cotton workpants. These pants became known as "genes." Eventually, the word morphed into "jeans."

🕊 Levi Strauss arrived in California during the Gold Rush, trying to sell canvas tents to miners, but he learned what the prospectors needed most were pants. Strauss spun canvas into gold by turning his tents into pants. They were a hit with the miners, but some complained the rough fabric chaffed. This caused Levi to switch to a wonderful twilled cotton imported from Nimes, France.

🕊 The cloth from Nimes was known as "de Nimes" or "denim." The term blue jeans finds its roots in the Nimes cloth that the Genoese dyed blue.

🕊 In 1885, you could buy a pair of Levi's overalls for $1.25. By 1900, the company charged $8.50 for a pair of their famous blue jeans.

🕊 What would you pay for the perfect jeans? In 2005, an original pair of 501 Levi's aged more than 115 years were sold to a collector for $60,000. Of course, if you don't have $60,000, you could just visit the Smithsonian Institute in Washington, DC. An original pair of Levi's jeans is part of their permanent collection.

🕊 In Spain, they are known as "vaqueros" or "cowboys;" in Danish "cowboybukser;" and in Mandarin Chinese "niuzaiku"—both of which translate literally to "cowboy pants."

B

Bones

 An adult has fewer bones than a baby. We begin life with 350 bones, but because bones fuse together during growth, we end up with only 206 as adults.

 The largest bone in the human body is the thighbone, or femur, which grows an average length of 19.88 in while the smallest is the stapes, the innermost of three tiny bones in the middle ear, sizing at 0.07 in.

 Hitting one's funny bone is the aggravation of the ulnar nerve, which runs near the ulna bone. This name is thought to be a pun, based on the sound resemblance between the words "humerus" and "humorous." The nerve was formerly called the crazy bone.

 The 2001 film *Bones* was a horror film set in 1979 and featured rapper Snoop Doggy Dog as a gangster who comes back from the dead to avenge his murder.

 A musical folk instrument called the bones was most commonly made up of a pair of animal bones—usually sections of large rib bones and lower leg bones—or a piece of wood (although wooden sticks shaped like the earlier true bones are now more often used). They have contributed to many music genres, including 19th century minstrel shows, traditional Irish music, the blues, bluegrass, and French–Canadian music.

Bourbon

🐚 Bourbon is the official spirit of the United States, by act of Congress.

🐚 The name "Bourbon" comes from a county in eastern Kentucky, which in turn was named for the Bourbon kings of France who had aided the American rebels in the Revolutionary War.

🐚 Bourbon County was in the early 19th century a center of whiskey production and transshipping (ironically, at the present time, it is a "dry" county). The local whiskey, made primarily from corn, soon gained a reputation for being particularly smooth because the local distillers aged their products in charred oak casks.

🐚 The A. H. Hirsch is a fine whiskey, smoky and complex, but the $120 cost is mostly for its rarity. It was distilled at Michter's Distillery in Schaefferstown, Pa., which closed in 1989.

🐚 This is how you would spell Bourbon in sign language:

B

Braille

❧ Louis Braille was born on January 4, 1809, at Coupvray, near Paris. At three years of age, an accident deprived him of his sight, and he was consequently sent to the Paris Blind School in 1819.

❧ Young Louis Braille desperately wanted to read, and he was only 12 years old when he invented the Braille system.

❧ On the dot! In Braille, any letter becomes a capital by putting dot 6 in front of it. For example, if "a" is dot 1, "A" is dot 6 followed by dot 1, and if "p" is dots 1, 2, 3, and 4, then "P" is dot 6 followed by dots 1, 2, 3, and 4.

❧ Research has shown that the fastest braille readers use two hands, and two-handed braille also seems to make it easier for beginners to stay on the line.

❧ The average reading speed is 125 words per minute, although it is possible to read up to 200 words per minute.

❧ A refreshable Braille display or Braille terminal is an electro-mechanical device for displaying Braille characters, usually by means of raising dots through holes in a flat surface. Blind computer users, who cannot use a normal computer monitor, use it to read text output.

B

Brooklyn

❧ John Augustus Roebling, who designed the Brooklyn Bridge, died of a tetanus infection after having his leg crushed by a ferryboat while working on the bridge.

❧ In early days, a part of Brooklyn was overrun by rabbits, which were often referred to as "coneys." In time, the area became known as Coney Island.

❧ Jay-Z's name was not only an homage to his musical mentor, Jaz-O, it was a reference to the J/Z subway lines that have a stop at Marcy Avenue in Brooklyn.

❧ Brooklyn (named after the Dutch town *Breukelen*) is one of the five boroughs of New York City. Located on western Long Island and an independent distinct city until its consolidation into New York in 1898, Brooklyn is New York City's most populous borough, with 2.5 million residents.

❧ The Dodgers baseball team originally hailed from Brooklyn. During the 19th century, because of the dangers of horse-drawn trolleys and carriages, the pedestrians of Brooklyn called themselves "trolley dodgers." Most of the working-class attendees had to dodge traffic on their walk to the games, so the baseball team named themselves the Dodgers in their honor. When the team moved to LA, they took the name with them.

B

Brothels

≫ In the 14th century, the term "brothel" was defined as a worthless fellow, a scoundrel, a "ne'er do well." The brothels consorted with prostitutes at brothel-houses and by the next century, "brothel" referred to the prostitutes and the house of prostitution. The word originates from an Anglo-Saxon word *breothan* for "going to ruin."

≫ The world's oldest profession may not be recession-proof after all. During the 2008 recession, top brothels worldwide suffered hits. Artemis, the largest brothel in Berlin, claimed its revenue had dropped 20% in November, a prime month for the sex trade. The multimillion-dollar Mustang Ranch in Nevada laid off 30% of its staff, citing a decline in high-spending clients.

B

≫ All aboard? Maybe not. In 2008, undercover detectives in Miami Beach, FL, allegedly paid a $40 entry fee to board a luxury black bus that contained women offering sex acts and lap dances for cash. The portable brothel had allegedly been cruising South Beach, a popular neighborhood among tourists and clubbers, before they were stopped by the cops.

≫ Japan's sex industry has a number of innovative variations on the brothel, but none of them are as perfectly, hygienically Japanese as "soaplands." These venues offer "assisted baths" that include the services of a prostitute. When a customer enters, he chooses his bathing companion from a selection of half-naked girls. A common service is for the girl to lather the customer up using only a little liquid soap and her naked body.

Buddhism

❧ Theravada is the oldest surviving Buddhist school. Founded in India, it is relatively conservative and generally closest to early Buddhist doctrine.

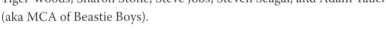

❧ Celebrity Buddhists include Oliver Stone, Orlando Bloom, Leonard Cohen, Richard Gere, Angelina Jolie, Tina Turner, Uma Thurman, Jet Li, Kate Hudson, Philip Glass, Courtney Love, K.D. Lang, Alanis Morissette, Sting, Tiger Woods, Sharon Stone, Steve Jobs, Steven Seagal, and Adam Yauch (aka MCA of Beastie Boys).

B

❧ Buddhism is the fourth largest world religion, exceeded in numbers only by Christianity, Islam, and Hinduism.

❧ The five precepts of Buddhism are do not kill, do not steal, do not lie, do not engage in sexual misconduct, and do not use intoxicants.

❧ Borobudur Temple, the largest Buddhist temple in the world, can be found near Yogyakarta, Central Java, Indonesia. The structure is made up of 55,000 square meters of lava-rock and erected on a hill in the form of a lotus, the sacred flower of Buddha.

Calligraphy

❧ Pat Blair, the official White House Chief Calligrapher, is responsible for the design and execution of all social and official documents such as invitations to state dinners, official greetings from the president, proclamations, military commissions, service awards, and place cards.

❧ The "write" stuff! Top calligraphers come together in Washington, DC, and demonstrate their talents at the annual Calligrafest, an all-day celebration of the lettering arts.

❧ Character sizes around 3 × 3 in are the easiest and most common in Chinese calligraphy. Characters smaller than 0.5 × 0.5 in require high levels of precision and strength from the artist.

C

❧ With a history of four to five thousand years, Chinese calligraphy was one of the traditional four arts (together with painting, stringed musical instruments, and board games) mastered by the Chinese literati during the imperial era. According to an old Chinese saying, "the way characters are written is a portrait of the person who writes them."

❧ "Nasta'liq" is the most popular contemporary style among classical Persian calligraphy scripts. Also known as the "Bride of the Calligraphy Scripts," this lettering style has changed very little through time because of its strong structure.

Calories

✒ The 2007 winner of Nathan's Famous Hot Dog Eating Contest in New York consumed a total of 19,600 calories and 1,280 grams of fat, which roughly translates to about 66 hot dogs in 12 minutes.

✒ Olympic gold medalist swimmer Michael Phelps consumed a *13,000* calorie diet during training. Breakfast: Three fried egg sandwiches; cheese; tomatoes; lettuce; fried onions; mayonnaise; three chocolate-chip pancakes; five-egg omelette; three sugar-coated slices of French toast; bowl of grits; two cups of coffee. Lunch: Half-kilogram (one pound) of enriched pasta; two large ham and cheese sandwiches with mayonnaise on white bread; energy drinks. Dinner: Half-kilogram (one pound) of pasta, with carbonara sauce; large pizza; energy drinks.

✒ According to a Harvard University study, children and teens consume 110 to 165 more calories than they burn each day. Over a 10-year period, that adds up to 58 pounds of extra weight.

✒ Americans today consume 20% more calories than a generation ago: most comes from fats and oils (up 63%), grains (up 43%), sugar (up 19%).

✒ A large White Castle chocolate shake in Louisville has 1680 calories.

✒ Negative calorie food is a term used by people who believe that certain low nutrient, high cellulose foods such as celery require very slightly more energy to digest than they provide nutritionally. Other negative calorie food includes asparagus, cauliflower, papaya, strawberries, and cantaloupes, but limiting your diet to just these foods would result in malnutrition.

C

Camping

🍂 In 2006, Daniel DeLaVergne, a world-famous whitewater paddler, was struck by a train while camping in a North Carolina train tunnel. Though he was airlifted to the hospital, he died the next day. The tunnel has 9 ft of shoulder room next to the tracks.

🍂 A "suitable pitch" is the term for a good camp site.

🍂 A south wind in the winter usually indicates a winter storm is approaching.

🍂 A "pudding stick" is a term for a short emergency or auxiliary paddle. It is a little one-handed paddle weighing 5–7 ozs, 20–22 in long, with a blade 3.5 in wide. Tie it to a rib with a slip-knot having the handle in easy reach, and when you come to a narrow channel, you can do anything with it!

🍂 "Giardia" is a microorganism found in unpurified water, and it can cause diarrhea, cramps, or other health problems. How do you recognize it? If the organism is split and stained, it resembles a "smiley face."

🍂 "Baffling" is the inner construction of a down sleeping bag used to keep the down from shifting.

🐦 If you ever find yourself confronted by a grizzly or polar bear who's making a non-predatory attack, play dead by lying completely flat on the ground. Lie flat on the ground protecting your vital parts with the ground and lace your hands behind your neck to protect it. Keep your legs together and do not struggle. Once the bear leaves your immediate vicinity, wait several minutes before carefully looking to see if the bear is still around. A bear may look back to see if you're moving. Remember: this is not applicable to all bears.

GRRRR...

Canada

❧ Canada is the word's second largest country, with an area of 9,984,670 square kilometers. That's slightly larger than the United States which is 9,631,420 square kilometers. Canada is over 40 times bigger than the UK and 18 times bigger than France.

❧ Hoop dreams…Dr. James Naismith, a Canadian, invented basketball while working in Boston as a means of keeping college students fit during the winter months.

❧ A fishy idea. Who else but a Canadian would have invented fish sticks? In 1929, marine scientist Archibald Huntsman invented "Ice Fillets," the first frozen food.

❧ Canada is an Indian word meaning "Big Village." The name Canada has been used since the earliest European settlement in the country and most likely originates from a First Nations word *kanata* for "settlement," "village," or "land."

❧ There is a town in the Canadian province of Newfoundland called Dildo.

C

Cannabis

🍂 In 2009, San Francisco Assemblyman and Democrat Tom Ammiano submitted a proposal which would regulate marijuana like alcohol. People over 21 years old would be allowed to grow, buy, sell, and possess cannabis—which is currently made illegal by the federal government. He argues that the taxes and other fees associated with regulation could contribute more than a billion dollars a year to state coffers.

🍂 Around the world…in the 8th century BC, Assyrians referred to it as "Qunubu." The Indians used it as an aphrodisiac, and the Chinese once thought that burning it as incense could lead to immortality.

🍂 The term "420" was coined in reference to the time of day that a small clique of kids at San Rafael High School in California used to enjoy getting high in 1971. The name stuck.

🍂 Cannabis has been used as a treatment for nausea, vomiting, anorexia, and weight loss in cancer and AIDS victims. It can also be used to decrease glaucoma, a condition of increased pressure within the eyeball causing gradual loss of sight.

🍂 Popular street names include pot, grass, reefer, dope, ganja, Mary Jane, weed, hemp, smoke, jay, hashish, dagga, and sinsemilla.

C

Cannibalism

🍃 Human sacrifice and cannibalism were widely practiced in Colombia before the Conquest. Two types of cannibalism existed in Latin America: *exocannibalism*, eating members of an enemy group, and *endocannibalism*, eating members of one's own group. Exocannibalism was a celebration of victory over an enemy, and the symbolic treatment increased enthusiasm for warfare.

🍃 In 1972, a rugby team from Stella Maris College in Montevideo and some of their family survived a crash of Uruguayan Air Force Flight 571 and eventually resorted to cannibalism. They had been stranded since October 13 and rescue operations at the crash site did not commence until December 22. In 1974, Piers Paul Read chronicled the story in the book, *Alive: The Story of the Andes Survivors*, which was followed in 1993 by a film adaptation called *Alive*.

🍃 On January 13, 2007, Chilean artist Marco Evaristti hosted a dinner party for his most intimate friends. The main meal was agnolotti pasta, which was topped with a meatball made from the artist's own fat, removed during a liposuction operation.

🍃 Carolyn Gloria Blanton, 54, who changed her name to Jane Lynn Woodry in 1999, has been under the care of the Colorado Mental Health Institute in Pueblo for well over a decade. She had been accused of shooting, dismembering, and cannibalizing portions of her former boyfriend Peter Green, 51, of Alamosa in late 1993.

🍂 Neanderthals are believed to have practiced cannibalism. The 100,000–120,000-year-old bones discovered at a cave site near the west bank of the Rhone river suggested a group of Neanderthals defleshed the bones of at least six other individuals and then broke the bones apart with a hammerstone and anvil to remove the marrow and brains.

Casino

🍃 All of the kings in a standard deck of playing cards represent real people. When the first deck was created in France during the 15th century, the designer used historical figures to represent each king. Charlemagne is depicted as the King of Hearts; Julius Caesar is represented by the King of Diamonds; Alexander the Great is represented by the King of Clubs; and King David of the Bible is represented by the King of Spades.

🍃 The same designer also used the suits to represent the different cultures that had influenced the world up through the 15th century. Spades, clubs, diamonds, and hearts represent the Middle East, Greece, the Roman Empire, and the Holy Roman Empire respectively.

C

🍃 It is still illegal to use slot machines in certain states of America which prohibit all forms of gambling. An individual can legally possess a slot machine if it meets certain criteria established by state law. For example, it must be considered an antique (at least 25 years old) and can be used for display purposes only.

🍃 The 10,500,000 sq ft Venetian Macao in China is the largest casino in the world. The resort has 3000 suites, 3400 slot machines, 800 gambling tables, and a 15,000 seat arena for entertainment and sporting events.

🍃 In Chinese culture, the number four is considered bad luck. Since the high-rolling whales from China are very important to the gambling industry in Vegas, the Wynn Las Vegas and Rio have no tower floors that start with four. The elevators count 38, 39, 50, 51, etc.

Castro, Fidel

❧ After the Queen of Britain and the King of Thailand, Fidel Castro is the world's third longest-serving head of state.

❧ Snooze-worthy? Castro holds the record for the longest speech ever delivered at the United Nations. On September 29, 1960, he spoke for 4 hours and 29 minutes. That's nothing compared to his 1986 speech in Cuba that lasted 7 hours and 10 minutes at the III Communist Party Congress in Havana.

❧ Castro claims to have survived 634 attempts on his life, mainly masterminded by the U.S. Central Intelligence Agency. The alleged assassination attempts have included the use of poison pills, a toxic cigar, exploding mollusks, a chemically tainted diving suit, and even a powder to make his beard fall out.

❧ Castro gave up cigars in 1985. Years later, he said "The best thing you can do with this box of cigars is to give them to your enemy."

❧ Though he was raised Roman Catholic, Castro never practiced the religion. In Oliver Stone's documentary *Comandante*, Castro states "I have never been a believer." He has total conviction that there is only one life.

C

Cats

• Cats can make over 100 vocal sounds, while dogs can only make 10.

• In 1879, thirty-seven cats were used to deliver mail to villages in Belgium. It wasn't long before they discovered that cats were not disciplined enough to do this.

• A normal cat has four toes and one dewclaw (thumb) on each front paw and four toes on each hind paw. Polydactyl cats may have as many as seven digits on front and/or hind paws, though it is most commonly found on the front paws only.

• As a revered animal in Egyptian society and religion, the cat was treated to the same mummification process after death as humans were. Mummified cats were given in offering to Bast, the cat goddess. In 1888, an Egyptian farmer discovered a large tomb containing eighty thousand mummified cats and kittens outside the town of Beni Hasan.

• A cat has about 19 million nerve endings in its nose, as opposed to around five million for humans. Every cat's nosepad, like human fingerprints, is distinct and unique to that cat. No two feline noseprints are ever alike.

C

Caviar

🐚 Italy and many other countries have banned beluga caviar, often the most expensive variety of caviar, in hopes of saving the dwindling population of sturgeon who produce the salty eggs. In December 2008, officials seized 40 kilograms (88 pounds) of Russian beluga stashed in the refrigerator at a home in Milan. The contraband delicacy was given to Italian charities to be served alongside the traditional foods they fed the poor on Christmas.

🐚 The word "Almas" means diamond, a fitting name for the world's most expensive and rarest form of caviar. It comes from 60- to 80-year old sturgeons and is a pale amber color. The only known retail outlet which sells Almas is the Caviar House & Prunier in London's Picadilly. A kilo of the rare caviar in a 24-karat gold tin sells for £16,000, or about $25,000. The Caviar House also sells an £800 tin for those on a smaller budget.

C

🐚 Several cosmetic companies have introduced caviar-based anti-aging creams into their skincare range. Since caviar contains a combination of proteins, low glycemic carbohydrates, and essential fatty acids, it allegedly stimulates the skin and improves the muscle tone.

🐚 Caviar is made by first removing the eggs from the fish and pressing them through a sieve to remove the membrane, fibers, and fatty tissue. The finest eggs are then mixed with a little salt and put into cans or jars as fresh caviar known as *malossol* (lightly salted). A coarser product known as *pausnaya*, which consists mostly of fish eggs that are premature or damaged in the sieving process, is more heavily salted and pressed in bulk. It is a staple food in Russia and Eastern Europe.

Cellulite

❧ Synonyms and slang terms for cellulite include "orange peel syndrome," "cottage cheese skin," "the mattress phenomenon," and "hail damage."

❧ Within the last 40–50 years, women went from loose underwear around the thighs to tight underwear going across the middle of the buttock. Underwear with a tight elastic across the buttock limits blood flow and thus encourages cellulite to form.

❧ According to its makers, the *MBT*, or the "anti-shoe," has a specially designed sole which simulates walking barefoot. This results in improved posture, a reduction of varicose veins, and diminished cellulite.

C   ❧ Cellubike, a machine that looks like the lovechild of a bicycle and spaceship, integrates cardio-vascular exercise with modern infrared technology to assist in weight loss and the reduction of cellulite. Infrared lighting helps penetrate the skin's surface to increase circulation, thereby helping the body remove fat on its own. The company also claims that calories are burned 10 times faster than regular exercise.

Champagne

❧ "I drink champagne when I win, to celebrate, and drink champagne when I lose, to console myself." *Napoleon Bonaparte, French military and political leader.*

❧ There are roughly 44 million tiny bubbles in a bottle of sparkling wine.

❧ A cork will escape a bottle of sparkling wine at 38–40 mph.

❧ Mon dieu! It may come as a shock, but champagne is an English invention. Fermentation naturally produces bubbles, but the problem has always been controlling them. The English developed a taste for the fizzy beverage in the 16th century, when importing barrels of green flat wine from Champagne and adding sugar and molasses to ferment it. However, it was the French who added the finesse and marketing flair to make champage. It wasn't until 1876 that they perfected the modern dry style, which, ironically, was for export to England.

❧ An age-old tradition is now becoming a common party trick at weddings, parties, and formal dinners. The "beheading" of a champagne bottle involves the use of a sabre to uncork the bottle. It originally began with the Hussards under Napoleon's command who celebrated their victories by "sabring" off the top of a bottle of champagne while on horseback. As legend has it, these skilled horsemen would ride on at a full gallop while ladies would hold up the bottles. In today's "beheadings," the horse is optional.

C

Cheese

🐌 "How can you govern a country that has two hundred and forty-six varieties of cheese?" *Charles de Gaulle, French General*

🐌 The first cheese is thought to have been developed around 4000 BC as a result of the Sumerian herdsmen storing their daily ration of milk in the stomachs of dried calf. The milk combined with the natural enzyme of rennin left in the stomach and then curdled, becoming cheese.

🐌 By 2000 BC, cheese had become a luxury item in Egypt, with recipes heavily guarded by priests. Kings were even buried with murals depicting cheese manufacturing scenes.

🐌 The average American ate 30 lbs (14 kg) of cheese in the year 2000, up from 11 lbs (5 kg) in 1970.

🐌 "Macaroni and Cheese" is the #1 cheese recipe in America. In any given twelve-week period, approximately one-third of the population of the United States will eat macaroni and cheese at least once. About half of all children in the United States will eat macaroni and cheese during this time period.

🐌 "Chasing the cheese" is one of the biggest social events in Gloucestershire's social calendar. The event takes place on Cooper's Hill in Brockworth, England, where dozens of people run down a very steep hill in pursuit of a massive seven to eight-pound Double Gloucester circle of cheese.

Chess

❧ The term "zugzwang" is frequently used in chess. A player whose turn it is to move, but whose move would serve to worsen their position is said to be in *zugzwang*.

❧ Chess originated in India during the Gupta empire, where its early form in the 6th century was known as "caturanga," which translates to "four divisions of the military" (infantry, cavalry, elephants, and chariotry). In time, these pieces evolved into the modern pawn, knight, bishop, and rook, respectively.

❧ Diana Lanni, one of America's top ten female chess players, used chess to beat a drug addiction problem and suicidal tendencies.

❧ Marcel Duchamp (1887–1968), the renowned French artist, was also a chessplayer who competed in the 1924 world amateur championship, four French championships from 1924 to 1928, and four Olympiads from 1928 to 1933. Of his marriage in 1927, friend and colleague Man Ray wrote: "Duchamp spends most of the one week they lived together studying chess problems, and his bride, in desperate retaliation, got up one night when he was asleep and glued the chess pieces to the board. They were divorced three months later."

❧ Russian serial killer Alexander Pichushkin was nicknamed the "Chessboard Killer" for murdering at least 61 people. He had hoped to reach 64 to complete the number of squares on a chessboard. After his arrest in 2006, the judge sentenced him to life in prison with the first 15 years to be spent in solitary confinement.

C

Chicken

❧ On September 10, 1945, a chicken in Fruta, CO, had its head chopped off...and lived for two more years. The axe missed the jugular vein and left enough of the brain stem attached for him to live and even thrive. Mike the Headless Chicken was featured in both *Time* and *Life* magazines and at the height of his fame, he was pulling in $4500/month and valued at $10,000. Chicken cha-ching?

❧ The chicken is the most common bird in the world. There are about 52 billion chickens worldwide, which is about nine for every human. 75% of them will be eaten.

❧ For 3,000 years, chickens were farmed primarily for their eggs. Only when the Romans came to Britain did it dawn on them to eat the bird.

❧ The "oysters" are two small, round pieces of dark meat on the back of a bird near the thigh, regarded by some to be the most flavorful and tender part of the bird. The piece is shaped like a small oyster, and has the flavor of dark meat with the tenderness of white meat.

❧ *Alektorophobia* is a fear of chickens. The victims are afraid of every physical part of the chicken, like its feathers, eggs, or any other contaminated body part.

❧ Some breeds of chickens can lay colored eggs—the Ameraucana and Araucana can lay green or blue eggs.

Chihuahuas

❧ Chihuahuas have *moleras*, or a soft spot in their skulls. They are the only breed of dog to be born with an incomplete skull.

❧ Chihuahua is a state in northern Mexico with a mainland area of 244,938 square kilometers (94,571.1 sq mi), slightly bigger than the United Kingdom. Although Chihuahua is primarily identified with its namesake, the Chihuahuan Desert, it has more forests than any other state.

❧ Famous Chihuahas include Boo Boo, a 4 in-tall, long-haired female chihuahua who weighs only 1½ lbs and was crowned the World's Smallest Living Dog by the *Guinness Book of World Records* in May 2007. Another famous Chihuahua includes Dinky, the first Taco Bell Chihuahua, who was succeeded by Gidget. Paris Hilton's frequently photographed Chihuahua is named Tinkerbell.

❧ Top marks for a top dog! In 2007, Maddy Yee earned the title as the fastest Chihuahua at the Petco-sponsored race in San Diego.

C

Chili

᪥ Arguably, the most famous bowl of restaurant chili was served at Chasen's restaurant in Los Angeles. It achieved worldwide notoriety when Elizabeth Taylor and Richard Burton dispatched a cable to Chasen's and ordered 10 quarts (frozen) to be sent to their address on Via Appia Pignatelli...in Rome, Italy.

᪥ Cincinnati-style chili is quite different from its more recognizable Texas cousin. It was created in 1922 by a Macedonian immigrant, Tom Kiradjieff, who settled in Cincinnati. His brother opened a hot dog stand that served Greek food. Since no one in the area knew anything about Greek food, Tom created a chili made with Middle Eastern spices. This "five-way" chili was a concoction of spaghetti topped with chili, chopped onion, red kidney beans, and shredded cheese. It's served with oyster crackers and a side order of hot dogs topped with shredded cheese.

᪥ The Chili Appreciation Society International has approximately 50 "pods" or clubs in the United States and Canada and supports over 400 sanctioned chili cook-offs involving thousands of participants each year.

᪥ Jesse James, the Wild West outlaw and desperado, refused to rob a bank in McKinney, TX, because that was where his favorite chili parlor was located.

᪥ By 1977, the chili manufacturers in Texas successfully lobbied the Texas legislature to have chili proclaimed the official state food "in recognition of the fact that the only real 'bowl of red' is that prepared by Texans."

China

❧ Traditionally, the Chinese have tested the effectiveness of herbal remedies on themselves rather than using animals. Emperor Shen Nung, who lived around 2800 BC, was the earliest known practitioner of herbal medicine and the godfather of Chinese medicine. He was reputed to have tasted hundred of different herbs in his quest for medical cures.

❧ Serbia's biggest Chinatown is located in the newer part of Belgrade though there are several Chinese-operated stores all over the country. A large number of Chinese migrated to Serbia after Slobodan Milosevic paid an official visit to China and relaxed immigration restrictions soon after.

❧ The story of Mulan had been told in China for almost 1,500 years before Disney decided to make it into an animated movie.

❧ Rice flour was used in combination with lime and clay to create a mortar used in holding the bricks together on the Great Wall of China. In some places of the wall, the bricks have eroded faster than the mortar between them.

❧ Lost in translation…Kentucky Fried Chicken's famous advertising slogan "finger lickin' good" was translated in Chinese as "eat your fingers off."

C

Christianity

🐦 Common symbols associated with Christianity include the cross, dove, anchor, fish, alpha and omega, and chi rho.

🐦 No one ever called him Jesus in his lifetime: it was a romanization of the Hebrew *Y'shua*, and the Romans used I's, not J's.

🐦 Pope Urban II (1088–1099) was responsible for assisting Emperor Alexus I (1081–1118) of Constantinople in launching the first crusade. He made one of the most influential speeches during the Middle Ages, calling on Christian princes in Europe to go on a crusade to rescue the Holy Land from the Turks. Any crusader could claim to be going on a pilgrimage for God and as an incentive, they did not have to pay tax and they were also protected by the Church.

🐦 The St. Mark's House in Jerusalem is thought to be the first Christian church. The Holy Spirit is said to have descended into St. Mark's house on the Day of Pentacost. St. Mark was martyred in 68 AD, tied to a horse's tail and dragged through the streets of Bokalia in Alexandria for two days. As a tradition of the time, parts of his body were preserved with his head now in a church in Alexandria and other parts of him in Cairo. The remainder is in St. Mark's cathedral in Venice.

🐦 The first Christmas cards originated in 1840. The letter "X" in the word "X-mas" is not used just to save writing out the whole of the word Christmas. X is *chi*, the first letter of the Greek word *christos*, meaning anointed.

Chupacabra

❧ The Chupacabra, a legendary cryptid from various parts of the Americas, is supposedly a heavy creature, the size of a small bear, with a row of spikes along its back. Sightings have been reported in Puerto Rico, Mexico and the US, but biologist and wildlife management officials view the Chupacabra as a contemporary legend. The name comes from the animal's reported habit of attacking and drinking the blood of livestock, especially goats.

❧ In Puerto Rico in March 1995, eight sheep were discovered dead, each with three puncture wounds in the chest area and completely drained of blood.

❧ Puerto Rican comedian and entrepreneur Silverio Pérez is credited with coining the term "chupacabras" soon after the first incidents were reported in the press.

C

❧ In April 2006, *MosNews* reported that a chupacabra was spotted in Russia for the first time. The beast reportedly killed 32 turkeys and drained their blood. Reports later came from neighboring villages where 30 sheep were killed and had their blood drained.

❧ In July 2007, a Texan rancher named Phylis Canion claimed she had captured a chupacabra. The creature had first started snatching cats, then two dozen chickens right through a wire cage. Canion claimed that the creatures were blue-skinned, hairless, and had strange teeth. Studying the DNA, biologists at the Texas State University announced that the remains in her freezer were not that of a chupacabra but, in fact, a coyote.

Circus

◈ The name "circus" was coined by an English trick-rider named Charles Hughes when he established his own ring in 1782 and called it the Royal Circus. Hughes took the ideas—which also included jugglers, trapeze artists, clowns, and animals—to Russia and there began the Moscow State Circus.

◈ The first building known as a circus was the Circus Maximus in Rome. It had been founded in the 6th century BC for chariot races and by the 1st century BC, Julius Caesar developed the stadium to hold 150,000 spectators. It was further extended in the 4th century AD to seat a quarter of a million people. The Circus Maximus was the largest seated stadium ever built. Only the ruins remain today.

C

◈ Vladamir Lenin, the Russian revolutionary, expressed a wish for the circus to become "the people's art-form," given equal status and facilities as a theatre, opera, or ballet. In 1927, the State University of Circus and Variety Arts—better known as the Moscow Circus School—was established where performers were trained using methods developed from the Soviet gymnastics program.

◈ Phineas Taylor Barnum (July 5, 1810–April 7, 1891) was an American showman and businessman who founded the circuses that became the Ringling Bros. and Barnum & Bailey Circus. Barnum dedicated his life "to put money in his own coffers." He was a businessman, his profession was entertainment, and he was perhaps the first "show business" millionaire. His last reported words were "How were the circus receipts today at Madison Square Garden?"

☙ Chang and Eng Bunker were Siamese twins joined at the sternum by a small piece of cartilage. In 1829, they were discovered in Siam by British merchant Robert Hunter and exhibited as a curiosity during a world tour. Upon termination of their contract with their discoverer, they went into business for themselves. In 1839, the twins settled in Wilkesboro, NC, becoming naturalized United States citizens. The best-selling and multiple-award-winning 2000 novel, *Chang and Eng*, by Darin Strauss, was based on the life of the famous Bunker twins.

☙ Ringling Bros. performers were notoriously superstitious. They considered sitting on the ring curb and the color green to be bad luck.

Clinton, Bill

🌿 Although he assumed use of his stepfather's surname, Clinton says he remembers his stepfather as a gambler and an alcoholic who regularly abused his mother and his half-brother, Roger, Jr.

🌿 In 1978, he became the youngest governor in the country at age thirty-two when he was elected Governor of Arkansas. After losing the re-election, Clinton once joked that he was the youngest *ex*-governor in the nation's history.

🌿 On October 17, 2002, Bill Clinton became the first white person to be inducted into the Arkansas Black Hall of Fame.

C 🌿 Clinton is the first left-handed American president to serve two terms.

🌿 As a delegate to Boys Nation while in high school, Clinton met President Kennedy in the White House Rose Garden in 1962. The introduction led him to enter a life of public service.

Coca-Cola®

❧ The predecessor of coke was an alcoholic drink called Pemberton's French Wine Coca, which was used as a headache remedy. The temperance movement caused John Smith Pemberton to create a non-alcoholic version of French Wine Coca, which he flavored using kola nuts. In the beginning, he only sold nine drinks a day at five cents per glass. A year later, in 1888, Pemberton sold his stake to the company Asa Griggs Candler. He also quietly sold it to three other businessmen. Candler eventually got hold of all the rights for the beverage and then burnt his records. A marketing genius, he made Coca-Cola® the world's best-selling soft drink.

❧ About 60mg of cocaine was used in each serving of Coke until 1903 when the company claimed to have removed the ingredient.

C

❧ The day before Martin Luther King was assassinated, he held a speech asking people to boycott Coca-Cola® and stop buying their products because of the way the company was treating black workers.

❧ It takes about 2.5 liters of water to produce just 1 liter of Coke at its bottling plants.

❧ In May 15, 1950, Coca-Cola® became the first product ever to appear on the cover of *Time* magazine.

Cocaine

- Yuegang Zuo, a UMass Dartmouth chemistry professor, did a study which detected trace amounts of cocaine in 67% of the dollar bills researchers collected in Southeastern Massachusetts within a two year period.

- As late as 1938, the classic French cookbook *Larousse Gastronomique* published a recipe for "cocaine pudding," a variation on zabaglione in which the traditional egg-sugar-and-wine mixture was boosted with extracts of cola and coca steeped in orange syrup. "Not only a very tasty dessert," commented the book, "but also an excellent medicine."

- Macadamia nuts are often used by law enforcement to simulate crack cocaine in drug stings. When chopped, the nuts resemble crack cocaine in color.

- Crack cocaine is a highly addictive and powerful stimulant that is derived from powdered cocaine using a simple conversion process. It is abused because it produces an immediate high and because it is easy and inexpensive to produce. The National Household Survey on Drug Abuse indicates that an estimated 6,222,000 U.S. residents aged 12 and older have used crack at least once in their lifetime.

- Robert Louis Stevenson was an invalid almost deranged by tuberculosis and the effects of medicinal cocaine when he spent three days re-writing *Dr. Jekyll and Mr. Hyde* by hand. The first draft was destroyed by the author's wife who dismissed it as a "quire full of utter nonsense."

Colosseum

❧ The construction of the Colosseum began under the Emperor Vespasian in 70 AD and ended during the reign of Emperor Titus in 80 AD. Unlike earlier amphitheaters, which were nearly all dug into hillsides for extra support, the Colosseum is a freestanding structure of stone and concrete.

❧ Archaeologists can't agree on an exact number, but estimates put the seating in the Colosseum at around 45,000 people.

❧ The Colosseum is located around 14 degrees North, and 43 degrees East.

❧ For four years, the death of men were a form of entertainment for the crowds. It began with fights to the death between wild animals, but later, there would be fights between men and tamed beasts.

❧ During the hundred days of the opening games, over 5,000 animals were killed, including elephants, tigers, lions, elks, hyenas, hippopotamuses, and giraffes.

C

Comet

🐦 In ancient times, without interference from streetlights or urban pollution, comets could be seen by everyone. Their sudden appearance was interpreted as an omen of nature and was used by astrologers to predict flood, famine, pestilence, or the death of a king.

🐦 Comets are composed mostly of ice and dust that grow tails when they approach the sun. All comets have a nucleus made of hard rock/ice. As the comet approaches the sun, solar energy begins to heat the ice and vaporize it.

🐦 The longest comet nucleus ever recorded had a measurement of 42 miles (67.6 km). The shortest comet nucleus measured 0.3 miles (0.5 km).

🐦 The first usable photographs of a comet's nucleus were taken by the European Space Agency's Giotto spacecraft as it flew close to Halley's Comet in 1986.

🐦 Compared to the solar system, comets are tiny. Like asteroids, they are bits of debris left over from when the Universe first started. According to one widely accepted opinion, comets are as old as the Universe and were once the blocks that produced Neptune and Uranus.

🐦 A comet can have more than one tail. The DeCheseaux comet fanned out like a peacock and had seven.

Common Cold & Flu

❧ In the United States, adults get an average of two to four colds per year, mostly between September and May.

❧ In November 2007, a mutated version of a common cold virus caused 10 deaths. Adenoviruses usually cause respiratory infections that aren't considered lethal, but a new variant caused at least 140 illnesses in New York, Oregon, Washington, and Texas, according to a report issued by the U.S. Centers for Disease Control and Prevention.

❧ A cough releases an explosive charge of air that travels at speeds up to 60 mph whereas a sneeze can actually exceed the speed of 100 mph.

❧ With only 30 seconds' of use, a handkerchief has been found to contain 15,000 germs.

C

❧ During the flu pandemic of 1918 (often referred to as the Spanish Flu), public gatherings were banned in some cities, and residents were required to wear masks. The epidemic killed 20–40 million people worldwide.

❧ Colds are caused by over 200 different viruses, and they are not the same viruses that cause the flu.

Confucius

~&~ Confucius translates literally as "Master Kong."

~&~ To ensure stability in his country, Qin Shi Huang, the first emperor of China, outlawed Confucianism and many scholars of the discipline were buried alive.

~&~ The Confucius Aristocratic Family Genealogy, the world's longest family tree by Guinness World Records, has documented a genealogy spanning more than 2,500 years. At last count, the total number of descendants exceeded two million people.

~&~ On study, "To study and not think is a waste. To think and not study is dangerous."

~&~ On ego, ""I don't worry about not having a good position; I worry about the means I use to gain position. I don't worry about being unknown; I seek to be known in the right way."

~&~ A state of Confucian...The terms "Confucianism" and "Confucian," derived from the Latinized *Confucius*, are western terms, coined in Europe as recently as the 18th century and bear no meaning in Chinese.

~&~ The *Lun-yü* (Analects) is the most revered sacred scripture in the Confucian tradition. Likely compiled by the second generation of Confucius' disciples, it is based primarily on his sayings and captures the Confucian spirit in the same way that the Platonic dialogues embody Socratic teachings.

Corkscrew

❧ The design of the corkscrew may have derived from the gun worm, a 17th century device that was used to remove unspent charges from a musket's barrel in a similar fashion.

❧ German Carl Wienke invented a single lever waiter's type corkscrew, which is still in common use today. The corkscrew was nicknamed the "Waiter's Friend" or "Butler's Friend," because it could easily remove and easily replace a cork.

❧ The vitual corkscrew museum at www.corkscrewmuseum.com boasts 33 "rooms" with 3,601 pages and 416 photos in the museum.

❧ On April 2000, Abraham Russel's January 21, 1862 American Patent No. 34,216 corkscrew sold on eBay for $13,550.

C

❧ In August 2006, the University of California, Berkeley displayed a 1,500-item corkscrew collection at the Phoebe A. Hearst Museum of Anthropology in Kroeber Hall, on the UC campus.

❧ In the movie *True Romance*, Christian Slater opens a bottle of wine with a Swiss Army knife corkscrew. It gets left on the floor and is later used as a weapon by Patricia Arquette.

Cotton

The word "cotton" is an English version of the Arabic *qutun* or *kutun*, a generic term meaning fancy fabric. Back in the day, a popular name for cotton was "vegetable wool."

Cotton seeds are tough enough to survive travel across oceans on the wind, which explains why similar varieties can grow thousands of miles apart.

Elvis, Sun Records, and the Stax Museum aren't the only things to come out of Memphis. The Cotton Museum is a historical and cultural museum that opened in March 2006 on the former trading floor of the Memphis Cotton Exchange at 65 Union Avenue in downtown Memphis.

Cotton has been cultivated around the world for more than 5,000 years. Interestingly enough, each country managed to develop similar tools to clean, prepare, spin, and weave it.

Cotton is also a food crop. Cottonseed oil is used in margarine, salad dressing, as well as feed for livestock and poultry.

The cotton gin is where cotton fiber is separated from the cotton seed. The first step in the ginning process is when the cotton is vacuumed into tubes that carry it to a dryer to reduce moisture and improve the fiber quality.

According to the Bureau of Engraving and Printing, U.S. paper currency is made up of 75% cotton and 25% linen.

Cowboy

◈ In 1905, William Picket became the star attraction of the Wild West shows his employers, the Miller Brothers, would hold at their ranch in Oklahoma. Bill later started a horse breaking operation near Austin with his brother. He was the first Black American inducted to the National Rodeo Cowboy Hall of Fame in the year of 1971.

◈ Feet first? Contrary to popular belief, the cowboy boot did not derive from Spanish or Native American influence, but rather, it's a direct descendant of a boot style made popular by Arthur Wellesley—the Duke of Wellington.

◈ The first Marlboro men weren't limited to cowboys. In the 1920s, Marlboro was first advertised as a milder premium cigarette for women. As the company sought to re-market filtered cigarettes to men, they advertised with all types of rugged individuals who smoked their cigarettes while performing equally "manly" tasks, from fixing cars to fishing or hunting.

◈ Annie Oakley was probably the most famous cowgirl of them all. Born Phoebe Moses, she was known for her sharp shooting skills by the time she was six years old. In fact, her shooting skills helped her parents to sell game to local shops and pay off their mortgage. As an adult, she was a sharp shooting star who toured with Buffalo Bill and his Wild West Show.

◈ Located in Fort Worth, TX, the National Cowgirl Museum and Hall of Fame is exclusively dedicated to honoring the courageous women of the Wild West who exemplified sass and spirit in their trail blazing efforts.

C

Da Vinci, Leonardo

- His first commercial painting was to decorate a shield, for which his father received 100 ducats...and kept to himself.

- Though the Mona Lisa was a commissioned project, Da Vinci decided to keep the painting for himself. After his death, it was bought by the King of France and remained in royal hands for more than two centuries. When the French Revolution changed the tone of the city, the masterpiece was transferred to its current home, the Louvre. However, Napoleon Bonaparte allegedly "borrowed" it for a while to decorate his bedroom wall.

- Da Vinci is considered by many to be the godfather of modern science. Though he is more widely recognized for his paintings, he was also a dedicated engineer and architect, designing many of the chief structures and public works of Milan. His scientific notebooks are filled with studies and analyses of problems in dynamics, anatomy, physics, optics, biology, hydraulics, and even aeronautics.

- He drew plans for the first armored car in 1485. In addition, he designed the cannon, a machine gun, gliders, a turnspit for roasting meat, irrigated canal system for fields, the parachute, scissors, and even invented the bicycle 300 years before it appeared on the road.

- Leonardo was born out of wedlock on April 15th, 1452.

- Leonardo was a vegetarian for humanitarian reasons—a very uncommon practice at the time.

Dalai Lama

❧ The Dalai Lama of Tibet, Tenzin Gyatso, is both the spiritual leader and head of state of Tibet. Born on July 6, 1935, he was just 2 years old when he was recognized as the reincarnation of the 13th Dalai Lama, Thubten Gyatso. He took the throne at age 4 and became a monk at age 6.

❧ The Dalai Lama grew up in Tibet's 1000-year-old Potala Palace in Lhasa. Since 1959, he has lived in exile in India since the Chinese Army crushed an uprising in his homeland.

❧ The Dalai Lama has a range of pastimes including meditating, gardening, and repairing watches.

❧ He has expressed a keen interest in science and has extensive involvement with research of how meditation affects the brain. He once explained, "If science proves some belief of Buddhism wrong, then Buddhism will have to change. In my view, science and Buddhism share a search for the truth and for understanding reality."

❧ Since he was a child, the Dalai Lama has always had an interest in machines. As a teenager he repaired a movie projector by himself without its guide or any instructions. He has said on several occasions that he would have become an engineer if he weren't a monk.

D

Dance

~&~ The risqué high-kicking cancan was considered too lewd back in the day and was banned from public performances in New York until 1866.

~&~ The Apache is a dramatic dance which some claim resembles a pimp dealing with a prostitute. The dance involves the woman being thrown about the floor by the man and ends with the woman skidding across the floor in an act of violence and submission. The name of the dance has nothing to do with the Native Indian tribe; but rather, it was named after a Parisian street gang.

~&~ Does tap dancing have you fumbling over two left feet? Try the slower alternative, clog dancing, which began in the 1520s in Lancashire, England.

~&~ Originating in Kentucky as a 19th century Shaker song, the Hokey Pokey is a group dance with silly words where participants stand in a ring during the dance and sing "You put your right arm in, you put your right arm out…" You know the rest.

~&~ *Best Dance Moves in the World* by Matt Pagett (Chronicle Books, 2008) features 100 step-by-step moves to tear it up on the dance floor—from Walking like an Egyptian to the Running Man to the more adventurous Funky Chicken.

~&~ The eighties produced many memorable dance crazes. For "Back the Bus Up," arms are stretched out in front of you with the hands in closed fists. Slowly walk backwards with small steps. Keep your head looking both ways and turn your hands like you're moving a steering wheel.

D

Daredevils

❧ Robert Craig Knievel, better known as Evil Knievel, was an American motorcycle daredevil famed for his stunts. He has several entries in the *Guiness Book of World Records*...including a record for 433 broken bones.

❧ Robbie Knievel is the third of four children of the late famous stuntman Evel Knievel and his first wife, Linda. The young Knievel began jumping his bicycle at age 4 and rode motorcycles at age 7. When he was only 8 years old, he performed his first show with his father at Madison Square Garden in NY. By age 12, he was touring with Dad and would perform in the pre-jump shows.

❧ Walk the line...In 1873, Australian stunt performer Henry Bellini began giving semi-weekly performances walking across the Niagara Gorge using a 1,500 ft rope, the longest ever used across the Gorge.

❧ Actor and stuntman Jackie Chan performs most of his own stunts, which are choreographed by the Jackie Chan Stunt Team. He has stated in interviews that the primary inspiration of his more comedic stunts were films such as *The General*, starring Buster Keaton, who was also known to perform his own stunts.

❧ In the 2003 film, *Daredevil*, Ben Affleck was cast as Daredevil after Kevin Smith suggested him to the director, Mark Steven Johnson. Like the famed character he was playing, Affleck was virtually blind while making the film. He had to wear heavy-duty contact lenses which blocked out most of his vision.

D

Darts

◆ The origin of darts is subject to debate, but one common claim is that bored British soldiers used to challenge each other by throwing their spears into turned-over barrel bases. Eventually they moved to cut-up tree trunks for targets.

◆ The late Jim Pike, a darts legend in England before most of us even threw one, was such a legendary marksman that he could shoot a cigarette from someone's mouth with a dart. Note: please do not try this at home.

◆ Singers Tom Jones and Englebert Humperdinck are old friends who often play darts together. During the 1970s, they purchased a 3,000-acre ranch and settled for the fishing rights by playing a game of darts. For the record, Jones won.

◆ Years ago, dartboards were made from elm wood. The numbers and wedges had to be carefully painted on and the spider (wires) had as many as 100 staples holding it to the board. To keep it from cracking, the careful pub owner would soak it in a bucket of water or spillage from the beer taps overnight. Soaking a loose dartboard in water will prevent darts from falling out but it will also ultimately shorten the life of the board.

◆ The average speed of a dart hitting a board is around 64kph (40mph).

Declaration of
Independence

❧ The actual Declaration of Independence measures 29¾ in × 24½ in.

❧ The original Declaration is exhibited in the Rotunda for the Charters of Freedom in Washington, DC. Due to the inadequate preservation techniques of the 19th century, the document is in poor, faded condition.

❧ In the last paragraph, the word "British" is misspelled as "Brittish."

❧ Apparently there are 25 known, original Dunlap broadside copies of the Declaration of Independence around—mostly in museums, the Library of Congress, etc. One copy, however, was purchased by Norman Lear and friend David Hayden, for $8.14 million.

❧ A rare 1823 copy of the Declaration of Independence sold at an auction for $477,650. In 2007, Michael Sparks found it while browsing through a Nashville thrift store. When he asked for the price on the yellowed, shellacked, rolled-up document, the clerk marked it at $2.48...plus tax.

❧ The oldest signer was Benjamin Franklin, who was 70 at the time. At the signing, he famously said, "We must all hang together, or, most assuredly, we shall all hang separately."

D

Diamonds

🖎 Diamonds are very valuable in the world of gems, but a top-quality ruby is usually worth more than a diamond of the same size.

🖎 Diamonds are typically yellow, brown, gray, or colorless, but other colors include blue, green, black, translucent white, pink, violet, orange, purple, and red.

🖎 The 545.67-carat Golden Jubilee is the largest faceted diamond in the world. It's a yellow-brown, brilliant cushion-cut stone, which was presented to the king of Thailand.

D

🖎 The Hope Diamond is a large (45.52 carat), deep blue diamond. It is legendary for the curse it supposedly puts on whoever possesses it. Previous owners include Kings Louis XV and XVI and Marie Antoinette. It is currently housed in the Smithsonian Natural History Museum in Washington, D.C.

🖎 The Taylor-Burton Diamond is a 69-carat diamond originally known as the Cartier diamond after Cartier Inc. paid a staggering $1,050,000 for the gem at auction. The next day, Richard Burton bought the stone for Elizabeth Taylor, which was renamed the Taylor-Burton diamond. In 1978, she sold the diamond to build a hospital in Botswana. It was subsequently purchased by Robert Mouawad.

Diets

❧ The earliest recorded 'fad' diet was followed by William the Conquerer (1028–87). William had grown so large that he confined himself to his bedroom, ate no food, and drank only alcoholic drinks. In 1087, at the Battle of Mantes, near Rouen, France, the strap holding the saddle on his horse gave way under the strain of his weight, and William died from the injuries he suffered as he fell on the pommel of the saddle.

❧ Dr. Robert Atkins (1930–2003) who was reknown for his cult "Atkins" diet, weighed 260 lbs at his death.

❧ Weight Watchers began in 1961 when an obese Brooklyn housewife, Jean Nidetch, tried to lose weight. She held meetings in her home to discuss ways of losing weight, and within a few months, people were lining up on the street to attend. In 1963, she created Weight Watchers and formalized the ideas that had developed from those meetings.

❧ The Apple Cider Vinegar Diet is simply the act of consuming 1 to 3 teaspoons of the tonic before each meal in the hope of losing weight. In the 1950s, a Vermont doctor named Dr. D. C. Jarvis wrote a book that established Apple Cider Vinegar as a weight loss agent. He claimed that regular consumption of the tonic would cause fat to be burned rather than stored. There is no evidence of its effectiveness.

❧ The Breatherian Diet promotes living off of the nutrients in the air. Scotland resident Verity Linn, 31-year-old Munich resident Timo Degen, and 53-year-old Melbourne resident Lani Marcia Roslyn Morris have all died while attempting to lose weight using the Breatharian "diet."

D

DNA

- Humans have 46 chromosomes. One chromosome can have as few as 50 million base pairs or as many as 250 million base pairs. There's an estimated 3 billion DNA bases in our genome.

- Our entire DNA sequence would fill 200 1,000-page New York City telephone directories.

- DNA is used to determine the pedigree for livestock or pets.

- Since 1989, there have been 232 post-conviction DNA exonerations in the United States. In 1985, Robert Lee Stinson was charged and convicted of first-degree intentional homicide based almost solely on purported matching bite marks on the victim to Stinson's teeth. He served 23 years behind bars for a murder he did not commit until DNA proved his innocence.

- DNA is strong as well as long. Under the right conditions, it can stay together for thousands and thousands of years. Frozen mammoths are a good example. In November 2008, *Nature* published "Sequencing the nuclear genome of the extinct woolly mammoth". The authors showed that about 80% of the woolly mammoth genome has been identified.

- In 1952, a tadpole was the first animal to be cloned. Before the creation of Dolly, the first mammal cloned from the cell of an adult animal, clones were created from embryonic cells. Since Dolly, researchers have cloned a number of large and small animals including sheep, goats, cows, mice, pigs, cats, rabbits, and a gaur.

Drive-Ins

❧ In Japan, "drive-in" refers to a rest area.

❧ In the German-speaking world, the term "drive-in" is often used instead of "drive-through" when referring to restaurants that offer those services.

❧ At their peak in the baby boomer years after World War II, there were more than 4,000 drive-in movie theaters across the U.S. Today, there are fewer than 500 still in operation.

❧ In 2003 and 2004, people began to organize "guerrilla drive-ins" and "guerrilla walk-ins" in parking lots and empty fields. The movie showings were often organized online, and participants met up at pre-determined locations to watch films projected on bridge pillars or warehouse walls.

❧ Starting in 1933, when the first drive-in theater opened, *Variety* magazine used the term "Ozoner" to describe an outdoor movie theatre in which patrons viewed a film from their automobile. The term was also used to describe the people that attend drive-in movie theaters.

❧ Richard Hollingshead Jr.'s motive behind the invention of the drive-in was actually to sell more auto products, as this was his business in the 1930s. He wanted to establish a place where people could park their cars, enjoy a meal, and watch a movie outdoors.

D

Drugs

❧ The first person to study the anti-microbial capabilities of penicillin mold was the French physician Ernerste Duchesne. As he was only 23 when he did his extensive research, the Institut Pasteur dismissed his findings. In 1912, Duchesne died of tuberculosis without his findings progressing any further.

❧ As early as 1829, scientists Johann Buchner of Munich and Henry Leroux of France discovered that an extract from the willow tree called salacin could provide pain relief for headaches. Unfortunately, salacin caused stomach inflammation and could induce vomiting of blood. In 1853, a chemist named Charles Gerhardt found a way of preventing stomach inflammation by mixing the compound with sodium, but he had no desire to market his discovery. In 1897, Felix Hoffman, working for the Bayer chemical company in Germany, rediscovered Gerhardt's formula and produced the product in powder form. Bayer created the trademark with Aspirin.

❧ Viagra, created by the drug company Pfizer, was initially used as a treatment for angina. Clinical trials failed to display any benefits for angina but reports noted that it had the marked side-effect of inducing strong sexual arousal in the male laboratory assistants.

❧ Human birth control pills also work on gorillas.

Druids

❧ Druids were not only priests, diviners and astronomers, but they were also judges, mediators, and political advisers who played vital roles in the declarations of war or peace.

❧ Druids were usually from noble extraction and trained from childhood. To become a druid required 20 years of formation.

❧ Druidism might have originated in Britain, but the Druids held their great annual assembly in the territory of the Carnutes, in central Gaul.

❧ Oaks were of primordial importance in Celtic religion, and the druids ritually cut mistletoe off oak trees. The word "Druid" is related to the Celtic term for oak, and the gathering place for Galatian druids was called *Drunemeton*, which translates to "oak sanctuary."

❧ Many Druids were women. The Celtic woman enjoyed more freedom and rights—including the rights to enter battle and divorce her husband—than women in any other contemporary culture.

D

Earth

 The Earth's shape may seem like a round ball, but it's much closer to an oblate spheroid—a rounded shape with a bulge around the equator. The bulge itself had been shrinking for centuries, but a recent study showed that it's now increasing. Accelerated melting of the Earth's glaciers is taking the blame for the gain in equatorial girth.

 Earth is a terrestrial planet, meaning that it has a rocky body unlike Jupiter, which is a gas giant. It is the largest in size and mass of the four solar terrestrial planets (Mercury, Venus, Earth, and Mars), and it also has the highest density, the highest surface gravity, the strongest magnetic field, and the fastest rotation. It also is the only terrestrial planet with active plate tectonics.

 In the 15th century, the accepted church dogma maintained that Earth was the center of the universe, and that the Sun, planets, and stars orbited around it. Any contrary theories and ideologies were likely to be seen as heresy by the Roman Catholic Church, and the perpetrator of any such theory faced being put to death by burning at the stake.

 One might say our Earth is thin-skinned…but it's all relative. The distance from the surface of Earth to its core is about 3,963 miles, but the solid skin of the planet is only 41 miles thick.

 Estimates vary, but roughly 1,000 tons of space dust enters the atmosphere every year and makes its way to Earth's surface.

Easter

❧ The origin of the name "Easter" is unknown, but a proposed theory by the 8th-century English scholar St. Bede is generally accepted. He proposed that it probably comes from *Eastre*, the Anglo-Saxon name of a Teutonic goddess of spring and fertility. Her festival was celebrated on the day of the vernal equinox, and traditions associated with the festival include the rabbit, a symbol of fertility, and brightly colored eggs, which represent the sunlight of spring.

❧ Traditionally, the Easter Season lasted for the forty days from Easter Day until Ascension Day but now lasts for fifty days until Pentecost. Easter also marks the end of Lent, a season of fasting and prayer.

❧ Eggs-tra, eggs-tra! The world's largest egg was produced by the Belgian chocolatier, Guylian. The chocolate egg was made with at least 50,000 bars, measured 27.3 ft high (8.32 m), and weighed 4,299 lbs. A team of 26 Guylian master chocolate makers made the egg over the course of eight days.

❧ According to the *Guinness Book of World Records*, Cypress Gardens, a theme park near Winter Haven, FL, landed the largest Easter Egg hunt title in 2007. With nearly 510,000 eggs hidden around the park, it took less than an hour for the eggs to be collected by eager participants.

❧ Easter is the second most important candy-eating occasion of the year for Americans, who consumed 7 billion pounds of candy in 2001, according to the National Confectioner's Association. It plays second to, of course, Halloween.

E

Ebony

◦ Ebony is a dense black wood, yielded from various tropical trees in Southeast Asia, but the term can apply to many heavy black woods. Because of its fine texture, smooth polish, and intense color, it's often used as an ornamental wood. In fact, ebony is used to make the black keys on pianos.

◦ Though it may seem that termites enjoy all wood, they will bypass ebony.

◦ The song "Ebony and Ivory" spent seven weeks at No. 1 on the Billboard Hot 100, and was the fourth-biggest hit of 1982. For Paul McCartney, the song's run atop the chart was his longest-running solo hit and for Stevie Wonder, it was his longest-running chart-topper.

◦ The wood of ebony sinks in water because it is so dense.

◦ Because they are so difficult to dry, ebony trees are usually girdled to kill them and then left standing for two years to dry out. After they are felled and cut into lumber, they must dry for another six months.

E

Echo

❧ Zeus, the King of the Olympians, was known for his many love affairs. Sometimes the young and beautiful Nymph Echo, who loved her own voice, would distract and amuse his wife Hera with long and entertaining stories, while Zeus took advantage of the moment to court the other mountain nymphs. When Hera discovered the trickery, she punished the talkative Echo by taking away her voice, except in foolish repetition of another's shouted words. Thus, all Echo could do was repeat the voice of another.

❧ Bats have developed the use of echolocation for navigating and hunting for food at night. By making high-frequency sounds, the echoes bounce back which enables bats to determine the size, location, speed, and even texture of objects in their path!

❧ "A duck's quack doesn't echo" is an urban myth! A duck's quack has an acoustic range similar to an echo and is subsequently hard to distinguish to the untrained human ear.

❧ No secret is safe…A whispering gallery is an enclosure beneath a dome or vault, where whispers can be heard in other parts of the building. Famous whispering galleries are located at St. Paul's Cathedral in London, England; Santa Maria del Fiore in Florence, Italy; and the Statuary Hall in the United States Capitol.

❧ In Hyderabad, India, the ruins of the once-stunning city, Golkonda Fort, can be found. It's been said that a perfect acoustical system had been designed at Golkonda. If one were to clap his/her hands at the fort's main gates, it could be heard at the top of the citadel, situated on a 300 ft (91 m) high granite hill.

E

Eclipse

🐚 Ancient cultures may not have understood the causes of eclipses, but they were often able to predict them. The gradual appearance of a lunar eclipse led people to suspect that something was consuming the Moon. In fact, the ancient Chinese term for an eclipse is *chih*, which also means, "to eat." The dark-blood color of most lunar eclipses confirmed the idea that the Moon was being eaten, with "blood" spreading across its face.

🐚 By February 1504, the famed explorer Christopher Columbus had been marooned on Jamaica for several months. Though the island natives initially brought him food, arrogant Columbus alienated them so much that they eventually stopped. As hunger and possible starvation set in, Columbus consulted his shipboard almanac and discovered that an eclipse was due. He called together the native chiefs and warned that if they continued to deny food to him, then God would punish them with a marked sign in the sky—he would darken the moon.

🐚 Arguably, the most famous eclipse of ancient times ended a five-year war between the Lydians and the Medes. The two Middle Eastern armies were consumed in battle when the day suddenly turned into night. The sign of this solar eclipse (recorded date is fixed as May 28, 585 BC) was enough cause to cease the fighting at once. They agreed to a peace treaty and cemented the bond with a double marriage.

🐚 A solar eclipse can last up to 7 minutes, 31 seconds.

Edison, Thomas

❧ Bright ideas…Edison has long since been credited for the invention of the electric light bulb in 1879, but this is not entirely true. In 1809, Sir Humphrey Davy in England connected two wires to a battery and attached a charcoal strip between the other ends of the wires. The charcoal glowed, making the first arc lamp.

❧ Edison is the inventor of the basic tattoo machine, still used today. In 1876, he patented the invention as the Stencil-Pens, which was intentionally designed as an engraving device. It was years later when Samuel O'Reilly made the world's first tattoo machine by patenting a tube and needle system to provide an ink reservoir.

❧ At the tender age of three, Edison was removed from school by his mother when teachers commented that he wasn't the brightest of the pack and "addled". His mother, so infuriated, began to home-school him instead. "My mother was the making of me. She was so true, so sure of me, and I felt I had some one to live for, some one I must not disappoint."

❧ At age 12, Edison started to lose his hearing. One rumored legend claims that a train conductor smacked him in the ears after he started a fire in a boxcar by doing experiments. Another states that it was caused by a bout of scarlet fever during childhood. The most likely reason is that it was a genetic condition since both his father and one of his brothers had impaired hearing.

❧ Edison earned a record 1,093 United States patents. His favorite invention was the phonograph.

E

Eggs

- Not only is the ostrich egg the largest in the world, it is also the toughest egg. It can withstand a person weighing slightly over 253 lbs.

- The least amount of spider eggs is laid by the Oonops domesticus, a tiny pink spider living in the walls of European homes. It only lays two eggs.

- The older an egg is, the easier it is to peel once it is hard-boiled. After cooking your eggs, you should also run it under cold water to chill the shell and keep it under the water while you peel it. It makes the shell come off more easily and prevents the greenish tinge from forming around the yoke.

E

- Generally, fresh eggs will lie on the bottom of the bowl of water. Eggs that tilt so that the large end is up are older. The tilting is caused by air pockets in the eggs that increase over time as fluid evaporates through the porous shell and oxygen and gases filter in. A rotten egg will actually float in the water and should not be eaten.

- Seeing double? Some hens will actually lay double-yolked eggs as the result of unsynchronized production cycles. A double-yolked egg will be longer and thinner than an ordinary single-yolk egg.

- Southeast Asian countries like the Philippines, Cambodia, and Vietnam, enjoy *balut*, which is a fertilized duck (or chicken) egg with a nearly developed embryo inside that is boiled and eaten in the shell…with a little salt. It is high in protein and is reputed to be an aphrodisiac.

Eiffel Tower

In 1925, the con artist Victor Lustig "sold" the Eiffel tower for scrap metal…twice. The Bohemian Lustig managed to convince French scrap metal merchants that the upkeep on the Eiffel Tower was so out of hand that the city could not afford its maintenance and wanted to sell the scraps. As the Eiffel Tower was designed to be temporary for the 1889 Paris Exposition, the idea was not entirely implausible. Lustig asked for bids to be submitted the next day, and reminded them that the matter was a state secret. He escaped with the money given to him by a man named Poisson, and nothing happened to him because Poisson was too humiliated to complain to the police. Lustig attempted to sell the Eiffel Tower a second time, but his mark went to the police and the story exploded in the press. Lustig was forced to leave Europe and head to the US.

In the 1980s, an old restaurant and its supporting iron scaffolding midway up the tower were dismantled. 11,000 pieces crossed the Atlantic in a 40 ft (12 m) cargo container and were reassembled in New Orleans, LO. It was purchased by entrepreneurs John Onorio and Daniel Bonnot, and was reconstructed on St. Charles Avenue, originally as the Tour Eiffel Restaurant and later called the Red Room. Today, it is run and operated by new owners as a training school for professional chefs and a banquet facility.

E

❧ During the Nazi occupation of Paris in 1940, the lift cables were cut by the French so that Adolf Hitler would have to climb the steps to the summit of the Tower. Allegedly, the parts to repair them were impossible to obtain during the war so German soldiers were instructed to climb to the top to hoist the swastika. The flag was so large it blew away just a few hours later, and it was replaced by a smaller one. It was said that Hitler conquered France, but did not conquer the Eiffel Tower. A Frenchman eventually scaled the tower during the German occupation to hang the French flag.

❧ The Eiffel Tower is painted every 7 years in 3 shades of brown (darkest shade at the bottom). Approximately 60 tons of paint is used.

❧ Fifty engineers and designers produced 5,300 drawings, and over 100 workers built more than 18,000 different parts of the tower in a workshop. Another 132 workers assembled them on site.

Elder Tree

🌿 Jesus's cross was made from elder tree wood and Judas, his betrayer, also hanged himself from an elder tree.

🌿 Elderberry, the fruit of several species of the elder, such as the American or sweet elder, is a roadside shrub found across North America. The berries are generally cooked and made into jelly or used for elderberry wine.

🌿 In Germany, one was to doff one's hat to an elder tree as a form of acknowledgement that it was the wood of the cross of Christ's crucifixion.

🌿 The fragrant flower heads from the elder tree can be used to make two delightfully refreshing summer drinks. One is the non-alcoholic elderflower press and the other is the slightly alcoholic elderflower "champagne."

🌿 The elder has long been used for medicinal purposes. Elderberries have been used to soothe winter coughs—a glass of hot elderberry wine can certainly soothe the throat. Apart from rosehips and blackcurrant, the berries contain more vitamin C than any other herbal extract. This may explain why Elderberry Wine is a potent remedy, especially when taken hot at night, for promoting perspiration in the early stages of severe catarrh, accompanied by shivering, sore throat, etc. It has also been hailed as an excellent remedy for asthma. Berry good, indeed!

E

Electricity

The US is the greatest consumer of electricity in the world using 3.892 trillion kWh (2007 est.) while China is a close second.

Electric eels can generate an enormous electrical charge to stun prey and dissuade predators. Their bodies contain electric organs with 6,000 specialized cells called electrocytes that store power like tiny batteries. When threatened or attacking prey, these cells will discharge simultaneously to release 600 volts of electricity—five times the power of a standard U.S. wall socket. Electric eels are not actually eels, and their scientific classification is closer to carp and catfish. Breaded and deep-fried, they would taste...electrifying?

Thales of Miletus (600 BC) found that amber attracted small particles when rubbed. In fact, that certain objects such as rods of amber could be rubbed with cat's fur and attract light objects like feathers was known to ancient cultures around the Mediterranean.

Static electricity is produced when one object takes negative charges from another object. Amber, a material created by fossilized tree sap, is a very good accumulator of static charge. For example, amber will become negatively charged when rubbed with wool so when a piece of amber is "charged up," it can pick up feathers and other light objects by electrostatic induction.

Elephant

🐦 Elephants suck water up into their trunks (up to 15 quarts at a time) and then blow it into their mouth. The trunk alone contains about 100,000 different muscles.

🐦 At Coney Island in 1903, an elephant named Topsy was scheduled to die after she had killed three men while she was helping to build Luna Park. Topsy was prepared by being fed carrots laced with 460 grams of potassium cyanide—and a current from a 6,600-volt AC source was then sent through her body. She was dead in seconds. An estimated 1,500 people witnessed the event and the film of the event was seen by audiences across the United States. It was directed by Thomas Edison who wanted to demonstrate the power of electricity as well as the dangers of it.

🐦 Unlike most mammals, which *grow* baby teeth and then replace them with a permanent set of adult teeth, elephants have cycles of tooth rotation throughout their entire life. Over their lives they usually have 28 sets of teeth.

🐦 Elephants are so clever! Not only can they play music, they also can be taught to paint. With their trunks, elephants can be taught to hold a paintbrush and through a series of commands and touches instructed by their keeper, they can create a finished piece. In 2004, one of these artistic elephants, Lankam, joined seven fellow elephants to create a record-breaking oil painting. Measuring 8 ft wide and 39 ft long, the piece was sold for 1.5 million baht ($43,000) to a Thai businesswoman living in California.

🐦 Founded in 2000, the twelve-piece Thai elephant orchestra at the Thai Elephant Conservation Center in Lampang, is the largest animal orchestra.

E

Elvis

🎵 Elvis Aaron Presley, born January 8, 1935 was an identical twin—his brother was stillborn and given the name Jesse Garon.

🎵 Following his separation from Priscilla, he lived with Linda Thompson, a songwriter and one-time Memphis beauty queen, from July 1972 until just a few months before his death.

🎵 Elvis was already a star by the time he was 10. He entered a talent contest at a state fair, donned a cowboy suit, stood on a chair so he could reach the microphone, and sang a version of Red Foley's "Old Shep." He won second prize, five bucks, and a free ticket to the county fair rides. In 1956, he sang the song again on his second album and the record went gold.

🎵 On December 21, 1970, Elvis Presley paid a visit to President Richard M. Nixon at the White House in Washington, D.C. Prior to their meeting, Elvis wrote to Nixon to suggest that he be made a "Federal Agent-at-Large" in the Bureau of Narcotics and Dangerous Drugs (BNDD). Despite the fact that no position existed, Nixon met with Elvis with desperate hopes to improve his image and win the love of the American youth.

🎵 Of all the requests made each year to the National Archives for reproduction of photographs and documents, the most requested item is the photograph of Elvis Presley and Richard M. Nixon shaking hands.

Environment/
Consumption

❧ Using the latest figures available, in 2005, the wealthiest 20% of the world accounted for 76.6% of total private consumption. The poorest fifth just 1.5%.

❧ If just 25% of U.S. families used 10 fewer plastic bags a month, we would save over 2.5 billion bags a year.

❧ About 1% of U.S. landfill space is full of disposable diapers, which take 500 years to decompose.

❧ In Peninsular Malaysia, more tree species are found in 125 acres of tropical forest than in the entire North America.

❧ New aluminum cans that are manufactured from used beverage containers use 95% less energy than producing them from virgin materials, the energy-saving equivalent to tens of millions of barrels of oil each year.

❧ Each year, Americans throw out enough plastic film to shrink-wrap the entire state of Texas.

E

Epitaphs

- "Workers of all lands unite. The philosophers have only interpreted the world in various ways; the point is to change it." Karl Marx, Highgate Cemetery, London, UK

- Rodney Dangerfield, the comedian and actor, died in 2004 from complications following heart surgery at age 82. A master of self-deprecating one-liners, his epitaph reads "There goes the neighborhood."

- Mel Blanc, the man who lent his voice to renowned characters—including Bugs Bunny, Porky Pig, Yosemite Sam, and Sylvester the Cat—died of heart disease and emphysema in 1989 at age 81. His epitaph marked a legacy with a dose of humor "That's all folks!"

- The life's work of Ludoph van Ceulen, who died from unknown causes in 1610 at age 70, was to calculate the value of the mathematical constant pi to 35 digits. He was so proud of this achievement that he asked that the number be engraved on his tombstone. So it comes as no surprise that his epitaph read "Ludolph van Ceulen: '3.14159265358979323846264338327950288…'"

- "Sir John Strange. Here lies an honest man. And that is Strange." This was inscribed on a tombstone of a lawyer in England.

- "Here lies Johnny Yeast. Pardon me For not rising." *In Ruidoso, New Mexico*

Famous Last Words

❧ *"Don't pull down the blinds! I feel fine. I want the sunlight to greet me."*—Rudolph Valentino, Italian actor and sex symbol.

❧ *"Either the wallpaper goes, or I do."*—Oscar Wilde, Irish poet and writer.

❧ *"Nothing but death."*—the response of Jane Austen, English writer, when asked "is there anything you require?"

❧ *"I should never have switched from Scotch to Martinis."*—Humphrey Bogart, American actor.

❧ *"I just wish I had time for one more bowl of chili."*—Kit Carson, American frontiersman

❧ *"I'm bored with it all."*—Winston Churchill, British Prime Minister, before slipping into a coma and dying nine days later.

F

Fangs

🐾 When brushing a dog's teeth, never use human toothpaste: it's too sudsy and contains too much fluoride for Fido. A meat-flavored toothpaste is available on the market or you can make your own concoction: half salt, half baking soda, slightly moistened. As for the dog's breath…

🐾 There is a dentist from Irvine, CA, named "Dr. Fang."

🐾 The clouded leopard, which feasts on monkeys, deer and pigs, has been discovered living deep in the Borneo rain forest. Its jaws can open wider than those of any other cat, and the fangs are as big as a tiger's, even though tigers are ten times larger than clouded leopards. Their two-inch canine teeth have drawn comparisons to the saber-tooth tiger.

🐾 The fangs of the tarantula are "hinged" to move vertically (up and down), while the fangs of other spiders move horizontally.

🐾 The gaboon viper of Africa is armed with the longest fangs of any snake in the world. The fangs have been known to exceed two full inches.

Feathers

❧ Birds may not be the only animals that can fly, but they are the only ones with feathers. Birds use their feathers to help them fly, to hide from predators, to keep warm and dry, and to display (or show off) to their mates or rivals. So you see why birds spend so much time taking care of their feathers.

❧ There are two basic types of feather: *vaned* feathers cover the exterior of the body while *down* feathers are located underneath the vaned feathers. The *pennaceous*, or contour, feathers are vaned feathers that arise from tracts and cover the whole body. Some feathers, *filoplumes*, are hairlike and are found along with the down feathers.

❧ An owl's flight feathers have a soft comb-like edge to help muffle sound.

❧ Snipe have two special tail feathers that vibrate during courtship, making a whirring sound called "drumming." I guess some could refer to this as a back beat!

❧ Feathers do eventually wear out and need to be replaced. This process is called a moult. As soon as a bird loses say a flight feather, another one begins to grow. Ducks prove an exception to the rule—they lose all their flight feathers at the same time, and they cannot fly for weeks until the new ones grow in.

F

Feminism

The term "Chauvinism" was derived from Nicolas Chauvin, a semi-mythical soldier under Napoleon Bonaparte. Despite the unpopularity of Bonapartism in Restoration France, Chauvin was said to be an ardent supporter and often donned a violet in his lapel, the symbol of his deposed Emperor. He remained fanatically loyal despite his poverty, disability, and the abuse he suffered.

Upon the death of her husband, female printer Anne Green became the publisher of the *Maryland Gazette* in 1767. She ran Maryland's only paper for eight years and when she died in 1775, her obituary read, "She was of a mild and benevolent disposition, and for conjugal affection and parental tenderness, an example to her sex."

"As one goes through life one learns that if you don't paddle your own canoe, you don't move." Katharine Hepburn, American actress

"I married beneath me—all women do." Nancy Astor, first woman to serve as a member of the Parliament.

Women in Switzerland weren't given the right to vote until 1971. 621,403 members of the all-male electorate voted for the female right to vote, while 323,596 opposed the measure.

Betty Friedan launched an entire movement with her book, *The Feminine Mystique.* Her analysis of women's role and status in society dramatically affected women in the US and internationally. She once stated, "A girl should not expect special privileges because of her sex but neither should she adjust to prejudice and discrimination."

Film

❧ Only three films have ever taken all "top five" Academy Awards; Best Picture, Best Director, Actor, Actress, and Screenplay: *It Happened One Night* (1935); *One Flew Over the Cuckoo's Nest* (1975); and *The Silence of the Lambs* (1991).

❧ The first film "blockbuster" was Steven Spielberg's *Jaws* (1975) because people lined up around the block to see the movie.

❧ In 1935, Dudley Nichols became the first person to refuse an Oscar film award for best screenwriter on *The Informer*. There was a union boycott of the awards that year.

❧ Lalita Pawar was a Bollywood actress with the longest running career. She was in more than 300 films over 70 years.

❧ Manoel de Oliveria was 99 and the oldest film director when he made his most recent movie in 2007. The Portuguese director has made a movie a year since 1990.

❧ "Film Gris," a term coined by Thom Andersen, is an offshoot of film noir characterized by leftist criticism of American society (1947–1951). The films came in the context of the first wave of the communist investigations of the House Un-American Activities Committee.

❧ An "orphan film" is a term for a motion picture work that has been abandoned by its owner or has suffered neglect.

F

Fingerprints

In Babylon from 1885–1913 BC, fingerprints were used as substitutes for signatures in order to protect against forgery. Parties would impress their fingerprints into clay tablets on which contracts had been written. Although the ancient peoples probably did not realize that fingerprints could identify individuals, references from the age of the Babylonian king Hammurabi (1792–1750 BC) indicate that law officials fingerprinted people who had been arrested.

In 1906, New York City Police Department Deputy Commissioner Joseph A. Faurot introduced the fingerprinting of criminals to the United States.

It remains the most commonly used forensic evidence worldwide—in most jurisdictions, fingerprint examination cases match or outnumber all other forensic examination casework combined. Fingerprints are reported to solve ten times more unknown suspect cases than DNA.

The fingerprints of koala bears are virtually indistinguishable from those of humans, so much so that they can easily be confused at a crime scene even with an electron microscope.

The largest AFIS (Automated Fingerprint Identification System) repository in America is operated by the Department of Homeland Security's US Visit Program. The archives contain over 90 million persons' fingerprints, many in the form of two-finger records.

Flowers

🦋 Spiderwort flowers have a very short life—only a single morning—after which the petals wilt and turn to a jelly-like fluid. However, each plant will produce 20 or more flowers per stem.

🦋 The False Hellebore or Indian Poke is a plant which grows in eastern and western America but not central. Native American tribes used it to determine their chiefs. If one was able to survive eating the very toxic plant (the roots and foliage are poisonous), they were worthy.

🦋 Low-pollen sunflowers have been developed in recent years which not only help asthma sufferers, but also extend the flower's life. Before the advent of modern materials, sunflower stems were used to fill lifejackets.

🦋 Pliny the Elder, a Roman scientist of the first century AD named the Gladioli flower. Struck by the resemblance between the sheath of the flower and the weapon that was carried by Roman soldiers, he called the flower "gladiolus" from the Latin word "gladius" which means sword.

🦋 The Rafflesia arnoldii, which can be found in the rainforests of Indonesia, is the flower with the world's largest bloom; it can grow 3 ft across and can weigh up to 15 lbs.

🦋 The Amorphophallus titanium has also been called the "corpse flower" for its unpleasant odor, which smells of rotting flesh to attract pollinators. The "corpse flower" is not a single flower but a cluster of many tiny flowers, called an inflorescence. The plant can reach heights of 7 to 12 ft and can weigh as much as 170 lbs.

F

Fly

🐛 There are over 120,000 species of flies ranging in size from 1/20th of an inch to well over three inches.

🐛 Flies are the only insects to have two wings whereas all other insects have four.

🐛 Entomologists Dr. Yao and Dr. Yuan of China studied more than 378,046 common houseflies and estimated that each carried approximately 1,941,000 bacteria on their bodies.

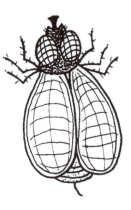

F

🐛 In 1923, black flies in swarms were reportedly responsible for the deaths of more than 20,000 sheep, horses, and cattle in Romania and Bulgaria.

🐛 Flies will only beat their wings when their feet are free. As soon as the feet become stationary, their wings will stop flying.

🐛 Flies taste, smell, and feel with the hairs that cover their bodies. The hairs on the fly's mouthparts and feet are used for tasting. Flies taste what they walk on. If they walk onto something tasty, they put down their mouth and taste it again.

Football

❧ The person with the most Super Bowl wins is Charles Hayley who was on the San Francisco 49ers from 1989–1990 and the Dallas Cowboys from 1993–1994 and 1996.

❧ The winner of the very first Superbowl was the Green Bay Packers in the year 1967.

❧ As of 2006, the cost of a 30-second commercial aired during the Super Bowl was an average of $2.5 million. The first famous Super Bowl commercial was a 1974 ad for Noxzema featuring Super Bowl legend Joe Namath.

❧ Joe Montana is the three-time Super Bowl MVP, nicknamed "Joe Cool" for his remarkable success in clutch situations and the postseason. Montana led the San Francisco 49ers to four Super Bowl titles from 1981–1989 and compiled a .713 winning percentage, third best in the Super Bowl era, during his 15-year career.

❧ Bill Hargiss is often credited with one of the first uses of the "huddle" while coaching the Oregon State Beavers against the Washington Huskies in a 1918 game in Seattle. It was popularized after a deaf player named Paul Hubbard began using it. To avoid having the other team see his sign language between plays, he and his team huddled together to conceal the signs.

❧ The first African-American player in the American League was Larry Doby with the Cleveland Indians in 1947.

F

Ford, Henry

🐦 Henry Ford called the Model T the "universal car," a low-cost, reliable vehicle that could be maintained easily and could successfully travel the poor roads of the era. By 1916, 55% of all cars were Ford Model T's.

🐦 Ford owned a controversial anti-Semitic newspaper, *The Dearborn Independent,* an incredibly offensive publication which damaged Ford's reputation. Hitler believed that Henry Ford was a perfect example for what all Germans should become.

🐦 As most people know, Ford produced the first assembly line for automobiles. He supposedly got the idea from a process that was used to slaughter pigs.

🐦 Though it owns a portfolio of British brands—Jaguar, Land Rover, Volvo—UAW Ford does not consider them American cars.

🐦 Henry Ford was especially fond of Thomas Edison, and on Edison's deathbed, he demanded Edison's son catch his final breath in a test tube. The test tube can still be found today in Henry Ford Museum.

🐦 Mahatma Gandhi never visited the U.S., but he had many American fans and followers. One of his more unusual admirers was Henry Ford. Gandhi sent him an autographed *charkha* (spinning wheel) through a journalist emissary.

Gandhi

- "The weak can never forgive. Forgiveness is the attribute of the strong."—Mahatma Gandhi

- Gandhi had a set of false teeth that he often carried in a fold of his loincloth. He put them in his mouth only when he wanted to eat. After his meal, he would take them out, wash them, and return it back to his loincloth again. An apple a day could have surely prevented the need for them!

- Gandhi believed in the virtues of a *Sativa* diet which consists of foods that are free of chemicals pesticides and artificial coloring. People who eat these natural foods—including fruits, vegetables, dry fruits, nuts, and seeds—are thought to think more positively, calm their minds, and help to energize their bodies and souls.

- As a lawyer in London, Gandhi got nowhere at all. He was practically a failure there. Years before, when he first came to England, his Irish teacher made him copy the Sermon on the Mount, over and over again, purely as an exercise in English. Hour after hour, Gandhi wrote, "Blessed are the meek, for they shall inherit the earth...Blessed are the peacemakers for they shall be called the children of God," and these words made a profound impression on him.

- His last words were *Hé Ram*! This is an exclamation to Ram (or Rama), who in Hindu traditions is one of the manifestations of Vishnu. Hé Ram means "O! lord Ram!". (This is invoking praise of Rama, rather than an expression of surprise.)

G

Gems

❧ There are more than 2000 different types of minerals, but fewer than 100 are considered beautiful or durable enough to be used as gemstones. Of these, only 20 are commonly used in jewelry.

❧ Hot hot heat…An amethyst will change its color when heated. Smoky amethyst stones can be transformed at temperatures as low as 250°F to a shining yellow or brownish-red. Clear amethysts, or those with a high degree of transparency, become yellow or colorless at 400°F.

❧ A star is born…A star sapphire is a special type of sapphire that exhibits a star-like phenomenon known as "asterism." These gems contain intersecting needle-like inclusions that cause the appearance of a six-rayed star-shaped pattern when viewed with a single overhead light. Twelve ray stars also exist, but they are much less common. The most notable sapphire mines in the US are located in Montana.

❧ In 2008, Los Angeles County sheriff's detectives found a stolen 370 million dollar raw emerald in Las Vegas. The Bahia emerald is believed to be the second largest gem of its kind on the planet and weighs an astonishing 850 lbs. It was stolen from the Pasadena, CA area; the robbers forged paperwork to remove the gem from a secure vault.

❧ Large quantities of a green mineral gemstone have been found on Mars. Rocky outcrops of the mineral olivine were spotted by a spacecraft orbiting the planet. On our planet, however, the mineral is more commonly known as Peridot, an inexpensive gemstone used in jewelry. Its existence on Mars suggests the planet has been cold and dry for billions of years.

Giants

🐦 The Bible tells of men of extraordinary size, called Nephilim, in the pre-flood world. The Nephilim were hybrid offspring of angels materialized into human form that had sexual relations with women on Earth (Genesis 6:1,2,4). The global flood of Genesis was said to have destroyed all life on earth which would include the Nephilim (Genesis 6:17; 7:17-21), however, in Numbers, some of the spies of Israel report that the Anakites, decendants of the Nephilim, were still living in Canaan (Numbers 13:28-33).

🐦 Saxo Grammaticus, for example, argues that giants had to exist, because nothing else would explain the large walls, stone monuments, and statues that we now know were the remains of Roman construction. Giants provided the least complicated explanation for such artifacts.

🐦 André the Giant was an actor and professional wrestler who began his career early at the height of 6 ft 10 in (2.08 m) and 6 ft 11 in (2.10 m). By the 70s, his height had inflated to 7 ft 10 in (2.38 m) but the height restrictions in the wrestling entertainment business (7 ft 5 in), forced Andre to keep his real height confidential. It was later announced that Andre was 7 ft 4 in with a weight that ranged between 460 and 540 lb.

🐦 When the Jolly Green Giant first appeared in television commercials in 1958, he did not exactly leave the desired impression. Kids were afraid of him because he looked like a monster. Del Monte worked on his image, added "Ho, ho, ho," and the jingle, "Good things from the garden" to soften his image.

G

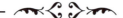

👋 David and Goliath is an age-old story from the Old Testament of a young boy who defeats a giant with a slingshot. In the early 60s, the Italians used the same character of Goliath as an action superhero in a series of Biblical adventure films. A 1959 Steve Reeves film, *Terror of the Barbarians*, was renamed *Goliath and the Barbarians* in 1960 in the USA. It did so well that it spawned a series of four more films including *Goliath Against the Giants* (1960), *Goliath and the Rebel Slave*, *Goliath and the Masked Rider* (1964) and *Goliath at the Conquest of Baghdad* (1964).

Ginseng

- Wausau, WI, is the ginseng capital of the world.

- Ginseng is an aromatic root that has been used for medicinal purposes in Asia for thousands of years. It has been reputed to cure cancer, diabetes, aging, sexual dysfunction, high blood pressure, and many other disorders.

- Soviet cosmonauts were issued pieces of ginseng to take along on missions into space as a preventative against possible ailments.

- Both the Native Americans and the early colonists used ginseng for a variety of medicinal purposes themselves. The colonists made it into tea to stimulate the appetite or strengthen digestion, particularly of elderly persons or physically underdeveloped children. A tonic made of ginseng, black cherry, and yellow root, and a tea of ginseng root and chamomile flowers were popular as well.

- A 100-year-old wild ginseng was sold for 1.88 million Yuan ($250,000) in an auction in Guangzhou, China, on November 6, 2007. Sure it seems like a pricey piece of root but not when compared with an earlier sale in August. That 300-year-old ginseng was sold for $400,000.

- Pregnant or nursing women or children should avoid ginseng. People with hormone-dependent illnesses such as endometriosis, uterine fibroids, or cancers of the breast, ovaries, uterus, or prostate should avoid Panax ginseng, Asian/Chinese or Korean grown, due to its estrogenic effects.

G

Glue

❧ Using "UHU Alleskleber Super Strong & Safe," a commercially-available household adhesive, the heaviest weight lifted by glue was a Ford Pickup truck suspended for an hour in Buhl, Germany on October 11, 2007.

❧ Neanderthals as far back as 80,000 years made glue from birch bark.

❧ The gods must be crazy...The oracle at Delphi had lent her wisdom to many events: she advised generals about invasions; and even warned Oedipus about murdering his father and marrying his mother. However, scientists now discovered that she was not blessed with prophetic vision. Rather, she was high from alcoholic vapors. The oracle chamber was built over a geological fault, which seeped ethane and ethylene gases. Consequently, the oracle, the temple maiden who uttered Delphi's prophecies, was likely in a permanent narcotic state.

❧ In December 2008, a doctor performed surgery on a three-month-old girl who had a vein of Galen malformation, or arteriovenous malformation, which caused her blood to flow too quickly from the arteries to the veins. He inserted a hollow tube containing medical glue through her groin and plugged the holes in the arteries. So by plugging the holes with the glue, Berenstein decreased the demand on her heart, which has already begun to repair itself.

❧ Elmer's glue is the glue of choice for students across the nation. It is estimated that over 47 million elementary school students use Elmer's Glue on a weekly basis.

God

🔖 The name of God is spelled with four letters in almost every known language. In Latin, it is *Deus*; Greek, *Zeus*; Hebrew, *Adon*; Syrian, *Adad*; Arabian, *Alla*; Persian, *Syra*; Irish, *Dich*; French, *Dieu*; Spanish, *Dios*.

🔖 The name God in the Anglo-Saxon language means good.

🔖 Huitzilopochtli was the Aztec god of the sun and of war. He was the patron god of the Aztec capital of Tenochtitlán, where Mexico City now stands. The Aztecs built a great temple there in his honor and sacrificed many humans to him.

G

🔖 Hurakan was the Mayan god of storms and winds. When the first humans made him angry, he swept them away in a violent flood. The word "hurricane" comes from his name.

🔖 The hit film, *The Gods Must Be Crazy* (1980), ran for 532 days in a row at a theater in Cupertino, California—the longest run of a movie in northern California. The only reason it didn't go for 533 days is because the film reels were damaged beyond repair and a section actually caught fire.

Golden Gate Bridge

- The Golden Gate Bridge has approximately 1,200,000 rivets.

- Closed encounters...The Golden Gate Bridge has been closed due to weather conditions only three times: December 1, 1951, December 23, 1982, and December 3, 1983. It had also been closed down briefly on two separate occasions for visiting dignitaries President Franklin D. Roosevelt and President Charles de Gaulle of France. Lastly, it was also closed on its fiftieth birthday.

- The bridge was the longest span in the world from its completion until the Verrazano Narrows Bridge was built in New York in 1964. Today, it still has the seventh-longest main span in the world.

- Only eleven workers died during construction, a new safety record at the time. In the 1930s, bridge builders expected one fatality per $1 million in construction costs. One of the bridge's safety innovations was a net suspended under the floor. This net saved the lives of 19 men during construction, and they are often called the members of the "Half Way to Hell Club."

- The Golden Gate Bridge's paint color is orange vermillion, also called international orange. Architect Irving Morrow chose the color as it blended with the bridge's environment.

- Suicide leaps off the Golden Gate Bridge are fatal 98% of the time. An average of 19 people a year take the jump, and the body count has clocked past the 1000 mark.

G

Golf

❧ Head's up! Wooden balls were used until the early 17th century, when the featherie ball was invented. A featherie is a hand sewn leather pouch stuffed with goose feathers and coated with paint. Due to its superior flight characteristics, the featherie remained the standard ball for more than two centuries. Since 1901, a one-piece rubber ball has been universally adopted.

❧ Dimples are put onto golf balls to eliminate aerodynamic drag. The drag acts as an anchor and the ball reduces in speed. Most golf balls today have about 250–450 dimples.

❧ In 1994, the year's leading PGA money winner was Nick Price, who earned $1,499,927. A decade later in 2004, Vijay Singh earned $10,905,167 as the year's leading PGA money winner, which made him the first golfer to earn over $10,000,000 in a single season.

G

❧ St. Andrews in Scotland is the world's oldest golf course and was used as early as the 16th century.

❧ The longest golf cart measures 6.68 m (21 ft 11 in) from bumper to bumper and was created by HSBC Champions.

❧ In the early days of golf, the clubs were much flatter and longer than they are today. They were made of ash or hazel and had a head made of apple, pear, beech or blackthorn wood.

❧ These days, full-length golf courses have 18 holes. However, until the mid 19th century, there was no set length and the size of golf courses varied.

The Great Wall of China

🐦 The Great Wall spans 4,000 miles from Shanhaiguan in the east to Lop Nur in the west, along an arc that roughly delineates the southern edge of Inner Mongolia, but it actually stretches to over 4,160 miles in total. At its peak, the Ming Wall was guarded by more than one million men.

🐦 Before the use of bricks, the Great Wall was built with Earth or Taipa, stones, and wood. Rice flour was also used to strengthen some of the bricks and mortar that make up the wall.

🐦 The purpose of the Great Wall of China was not only built to keep out the Huns from the north, but also to prevent them from bringing their horses across. Without their horses, they weren't very effective warriors.

🐦 The Great Wall is thought to be a single structure when in fact it is not. It actually consists of numerous walls built by different dynasties over more than 2,000 years.

🐦 In every marathon, there is the psychological barrier of "hitting the wall." In the Great Wall Marathon, the course takes runners through rural villages surrounding the wall and at least 4 miles on the actual wall. On Saturday May 17, 2008, The Great Wall Marathon® supported over 1700 runners from 49 countries.

G

Gutenberg, Johann

❧ Johann Gutenberg, a German, invented the printing press in the 1450s. It made new ideas available to a much larger audience and thus allowed the Renaissance to spread.

❧ Johann Gutenberg was a German goldsmith. In those days, people laboriously copied books by hand or printed them from wooden blocks where each letter of every page was carved individually. Gutenberg learned to make metal letters that he called "type." He could pick up the letters and place them in rows to build pages. A frame held each page together. Gutenberg fixed the frame to a press and pressed the inky surface of his type onto sheets of paper. Gutenberg's movable type helped him to make copies of books faster and more cheaply than ever before. Surprisingly, despite the importance of his achievement, he never made much money from it.

❧ The *Gutenberg Bible* was completed between 1450 and 1455. Early documentation states that a total of 200 copies were scheduled for print on rag cotton linen paper and 30 copies on vellum animal skin—though there is no record of how many copies were actually printed. Today, only 22 copies are known to exist, 7 of which are on vellum.

❧ Though it remains to be seen, an entire *Gutenberg Bible* is valued at an estimated 100 million dollars. An individual leaf (a single two-sided page) from the original *Gutenberg Bible* can bring in around $100,000. Gutenberg's work is the most rare and valuable printed material in the world.

G

Handcuffs

- The English word "handcuff" is a corruption of the Anglo-Saxon word *handcops*, an obsolete word meaning "to fetter."

- In February 2008, an eight-year-old boy in New Hampshire had to be freed by firefighters after getting stuck in a pair of handcuffs he found in his mother's bedroom.

- For over 15 years TUFF-TIES, plastic disposable handcuffs, have been used and approved internationally by the Military and over 3,000 federal, state, county, local police agencies, and security forces in all types of arrest and restraint situations.

- A standard pair of modern handcuffs weighs no more than 15 oz and the minimum opening of the bracelet is 2 inches. The maximum overall length of the handcuffs is 9.4 in (24 cm).

- Some might say she was served…twice. Jean Merola, a 75-year-old grandmother of eight, was arrested for disorderly conduct after she refused an officer's orders to move her car while she waited for the coffee and fries she ordered at the drive-through window. Merola was handcuffed behind her back and put in the cruiser.

- In 1910, Houdini published the book *Handcuff Secrets* to discourage hack imitators. In the book, he wrote, "you can open the majority of the old-time cuffs with a shoestring. By simply making a loop in the string, you can lasso the end of the screw in the lock and yank the bolt back, and so open the cuff in as clean a manner as if opened with the original key."

Helium

◆ Helium is the second lightest element and next to hydrogen, it is the second most abundant in the universe. In fact, all natural gas contains some traceable quantity of helium.

◆ In 1965, helium use in the United States was more than eight times the peak wartime consumption.

◆ Helium is a very light, inert, colorless gas and has the lowest melting point of any element. No matter how low the temperature, helium is the only liquid that cannot be solidified and remains a liquid to absolute zero.

◆ Helium is often mixed with oxygen for deep sea diving to help reduce the effects of narcosis. The mixture is called cold heliox.

H

Henry VIII

❧ Henry's attempt to have his 24-year marriage to Catherine of Aragon annulled set in motion a chain of events that led to England's break with the Roman Catholic Church. It also lead him to marry Anne Boleyn on the judgment of clergy in England, without reference to the Pope. Anne was consequently crowned queen consort on June 1, 1533. She gave birth to Elizabeth on September 7, 1533.

❧ Henry was an avid gambler and a fan of dice playing.

❧ He was also quite the womanizer. He had several mistresses, and at least one illegitimate son, Henry Fitzroy, who was given the title Duke of Richmond and Somerset. One of Henry's mistresses was Mary Boleyn, sister of Anne Boleyn.

H

❧ In his early life he enjoyed physical activities including hunting, hawking, horseback riding, jousting, tennis, archery, and wrestling. He was also well-educated and intelligent and enjoyed writing and composing music. Henry loved court life with its pageants, dancing and masques. After a leg injury gave rise to an ulcer in his later life, Henry indulged in eating and drinking to become large and bloated.

❧ His dying words were supposed to be "Monks, Monks, Monks!"

Hiccups

❧ Hiccups are also known as "singulitis." The American Cancer Society reports that 30% of chemotherapy patients suffer singulitis as a side effect of treatment.

❧ Though nobody knows for sure why we hiccup, one theory suggests that it was a handy function to have when we first evolved to air-breathing lungs, as we also had gills.

❧ Hiccups are treated medically in severe cases only. One such case occurred in 2007 when a 15-year-old girl hiccupped continuously for five weeks.

❧ American man Charles Osborne had the hiccups for 68 years, from 1922 to 1990, and earned himself the Guinness World Record as the man with the Longest Attack of Hiccups. The hiccups began in 1922 at a rate of 40 times per minute, slowing to 20 hiccups per minute and eventually stopping on June 5, 1990, a total of 68 years.

❧ Ultrasound scans show that two-month-old babies hiccup in the womb, before any breathing movements appear.

H

Hieroglyphs

🐚 The Rosetta stone was made up of three different languages: one single passage had two Egyptian language scripts (Hieroglyphic and Demotic) and one in classical Greek. Jean-François Champollion who finally deciphered it stated, "It is a complex system, writing figurative, symbolic, and phonetic all at once, in the same text, the same phrase, I would almost say in the same word."

🐚 One of the most interesting facts about hieroglyphs is that one symbol alone could have up to three meanings and could be either phonetic or simply a representative of the picture it depicted.

🐚 Hieroglyphs could be written left to right, up and down, or right to left.

🐚 Honey dates back for 150 million years, and it's written about in hieroglyphics. Egyptians would use honey as a form of payment, like the Aztecs used cocoa beans.

🐚 Each Pharaoh had his own hieroglyph. When the Pharaoh died, his mummy would have a nametag with his hieroglyph symbol on it, identifying the mummy.

Himalayas

- When translated, the Himalayas means the "abode of snow."

- 70 million years ago, a tremendous collision between India and Asia (via the Indo Australian and Eurasian plates) occurred, and the Himalayas were born.

- The largest lake in the Himalayas is the Pangong Tso, which is spread across the border between India and Tibet. It is situated at an altitude of 4,600 m and is 8 km wide and nearly 134 km long.

- 75% of Nepal is covered by the Himalayas.

- Mount Everest (8,848 meters), the highest mountain in the world, is part of the Himalayas in Nepal.

- Edmund Hillary and Tenzing Norgay were the first people to climb Mount Everest in 1953.

- When climbing Mount Everest, low air pressure in the high altitudes means less oxygen. Once a climber reaches 10,000 ft, they must remain at that height for three days, so their body acclimates to the decrease in oxygen. Many climbers can suffer from disturbed sleep, headaches and dizziness, though these symptoms generally subside within three days. Severe acute mountain sickness can occur when a climber ascends too quickly because a lack of oxygen causes fluid to leak from the blood vessels into the brain or the lungs. This eventually causes shortness of breath, confusion, loss of co-ordination, and hallucinations.

H

Honey

🐝 Honey is the main ingredient in the alcoholic beverage mead, which is also known as "honey wine" or "honey beer" (although it is neither wine nor beer, respectively).

🐝 Beer that is brewed with more than 30% honey as a source of sugar by weight is known as braggot.

🐝 Burying the dead (especially nobility) in or with honey was common practice in Egypt, Assyria, and other regions. Honey was also used to embalm the dead.

🐝 Apitherapy is the medical use of honey bee products, which includes honey, pollen, propolis, royal jelly, and bee venom. The American Apitherapy Society states that bee venom is beneficial for a variety of problems such as eczema, psoriasis, warts, laryngitis, emphysema, asthma, and glaucoma.

🐝 Historically, honey was used as a salve, either alone or mixed with fat. Because of its antibiotic properties and high sugar content, it was said to heal dead tissues and ulcers. Honey was often used to treat gun shot wounds not only because of its bactericidal properties, but also because the consistency prohibited air and irritants from entering the wound, and in many cases it was more accessible than other forms of treatment. Honey has even been used in hospitals as a dressing for wounds, burns, and cuts.

Hot Dogs

🍴 7-Eleven is North America's number-one retailer of fresh-grilled hot dogs, selling approximately 100 million each year.

🍴 The frankfurter originated in Germany, but the hot dog gained popularity in the U.S. more than 100 years ago under the nickname "dachshund's sausage." It was dubbed "hot dog" by the cartoonist T.A. "Tad" Dorgan in 1906. He depicted a dachshund inside an elongated bun as a character in his comic strip, and the name stuck.

🍴 When King George VI of England visited the United States in 1939, no expense was spared—President Franklin D. Roosevelt served him hot dogs and beer. When Queen Elizabeth II held a royal banquet for the American Bar Association in 1957, she included hot dogs on the menu. And, First Lady Rosalynn Carter continued the tradition when she served hot dogs at a White House picnic in 1977.

🍴 Mickey Mouse's first words were "hot dogs" which he said out loud (obviously) in the 1929 short *The Karnival Kid*.

🍴 The World's Longest Hot Dog created was 60 m (196.85 ft), and rested within a 60.3 m (198 ft) bun. The hot dog was prepared by Shizuoka Meat Producers for the All-Japan Bread Association, which baked the bun and coordinated the event, including official measurement for the world record. The giant dog was the highlight of a media event, which celebrated the Association's 50th anniversary on August 4, 2006 in Tokyo, Japan.

H

Hula Hoop

- Greatest number of hula-hoops caught and spun was 236 performed by Liu Rongrong of China in September 2007.

- Native Americans used hoops as a target for teaching hunting accuracy.

- The word "hula" was added in the early 18th century when sailors who visited Hawaii noticed the similarity between hula dancing and tripping hoops.

- After the hoop was released in 1958, the company Wham-O sold 25 million in the first four months and over 100 million in its first year. As the fad ran its course, Wham-O again struck gold with the release of a flying disc known as a Frisbee.

- The largest hula-hoop on record is 52.8 ft in diameter. Roman Schedler of Austria spun this hoop for 15:21 minutes on September 9, 1999.

Human Brain

● Early man practiced brain surgery since Neolithic times, and Hippocrates himself left copious notes on how to treat head injuries and depression.

● The color blue causes the brain to release calming hormones.

● At the time of birth, the size of the brain is approximately 400gms while the adult brain is approximately 1400gms.

● The height of an adult brain measures 3.6 in; length 6.3 in; and width 5.5 in.

● A small area in the brain called the *amygdala* is responsible for your ability to read someone else's face for clues to how they are feeling.

● Information transmits at different speeds within different types of neurons—it can be as slow as 0.5 meters per second or as fast as 120 meters per second.

● 750ml of blood pumps through the brain every minute.

H

Human Heart

- The human heart can create enough pressure to squirt blood at a distance of 30 ft.

- In a lifetime, the heart pumps about one million barrels of blood.

- In 1707, medical pioneer John Flower of Staffordshire, invented a stopwatch to measure the human pulse.

- The aorta has a diameter similar to a garden hose. Capillaries on the other hand are incredibly thin; it takes 10 of them to equal the diameter of a human hair.

- The human heart beats about 100,000 times each day and about 35 million times in a year. The heart, during an average life span, will beat more than 2.5 billion times.

- The first human-to-human heart transplant was in 1967. In Cape Town, South Africa, Dr. Christian Barnard successfully transplanted the heart of an 18-year old car accident victim into Louis Washkansky. Washkansky only lived for 18 days before dying of pneumonia.

Ice Cream

❧ In the first century AD, the Roman Emperor Nero developed a taste for a frozen dessert. He ordered runners to pass buckets of snow from the mountains along the Appian Way down to Rome. The snow was flavored with red wine and honey to be served at banquets.

❧ The Chinese may have been the inventors of ice cream. In the first millennium AD, Marco Polo returned to Venice from his trip to the Far East, with ancient recipes for concoctions made of snow, fruit juice, and fruit pulp.

❧ I scream, you scream, we all scream for ice cream…In 1984, President Ronald Reagan officially designated July as National Ice Cream Month and the third Sunday of the month would be celebrated as National Ice Cream Day. More ice cream is sold on Sunday than any other day of the week.

❧ Wall's was the first company to sell ice cream from tricycles. In 1924, this new marketing concept was launched with the slogan "Stop me and buy one." To "equalize the seasonality," the Wall's company would complement their summer ice-cream season with a winter sausage one.

❧ The top five most popular ice-cream flavors in the U.S. are vanilla, chocolate, Neapolitan, strawberry, and cookies n' cream, in that order. Vanilla accounts for nearly ¼ of all sales.

❧ In 1924, the average American ate eight pints a year. According to the International Dairy Foods Association, the figure had jumped to 48 pints a year by 1997.

Iceland

- Vigdís Finnbogadóttir, president of Iceland from 1980 to 1996, was the world's first female president.

- Iceland, like Hawaii, was formed by volcanoes. When the Askja volcano erupted in 1875, it caused massive devastation including widespread famine and a crushed economy.

- Iceland's flag's coloring depicts a vision of the nation's landscape. Red is the fire produced by the volcanoes, white reflects the ice and snow, and blue is for the Atlantic Ocean.

- Though one might believe that Bjork has the country's fastest-selling records of all time, the honor actually goes to an opera singer by the name of Gardar Thor Cortes.

- The Icelandic word "bjork" translates to birch tree and is a common name for Scandinavian girls.

- Open arms…Iceland is not a member of the EU and has no armed forces. In 1985, it declared itself a nuclear-free zone.

- Iceland boasts 10,000 waterfalls, 5 glaciers, 15 active volcanoes, and more than 10 million puffins.

- Most Icelanders do not have a surname (i.e. Johnson or Smith). Rather, the children adopt the father's given name. For example, Jon's son would be called Thor Jonsson and his daughter would be called Hadis Jonsdottir.

India

🍃 The name "India" originates from the River Indus, the surrounding valleys which were the home of the early settlers. The Aryan worshippers referred to the river Indus as the Sindhu.

🍃 India is second only to China in country population. It's growing by approximately 17 million people a year and could potentially surpass China by 2030.

🍃 Bollywood, the Mumbai-based production empire, is the largest film industry in the world…including Hollywood.

🍃 Martial Arts were first created in India, and later spread to Asia by Buddhist missionaries.

🍃 Yoga has existed for more than 5,000 years in India.

🍃 Our counting system was actually invented in India, then borrowed and popularized by the Arabs.

🍃 Nek Chand Saini, of Chandigarh, India, has created over 20,000 sculptures, waterfalls, and bridges around his home using old car parts, light bulbs and bicycle frames.

I

Insomnia

 The art of sleep proved challenging for Vincent van Gogh. He could only sleep by smothering his mattress and pillow with camphor to clear his mind of all his strange thoughts.

 The Earl of Rosebery (Prime Minister of England 1894–1895) was forced to resign from his position due to his chronic insomnia.

 Insomnia is more common among the elderly and women, especially after menopause.

 Not only does insomnia affect concentration and focus, it can cause irritability, impaired motor skills, exhaustion, impaired memory, blurry vision, stress intolerance, constant appetite changes, and discomfort.

 Fatal familial insomnia (FFI) is a very rare disease of the brain, which has been found in just 28 families worldwide. If one parent has the gene, the child has a 50% chance of inheriting it. The patient's progression into complete sleeplessness is incurable, and ultimately fatal.

 Sleepless in Sea…Research has revealed that newborn dolphins and killer whales can forego sleep for their entire first month. Both species of the mammals can remain active 24/7 for weeks after birth.

Internet

❧ The forerunner of the Internet was the ARPAnet—the ARPA stands for Advanced Research Projects Agency, a division of the US Defense Department that possessed linked computers across North America, and used them to exchange information. ARPAnet was planned in 1966, started working in 1969 but ceased operations by 1990.

❧ Video artist Nam June Paik coined the phrase "information superhighway" in a 1974 study for the Rockefeller Foundation.

❧ Google's name is a play on the word "googol," which refers to the number 1 followed by one hundred zeroes. Google's play on the term reflects the company's mission to organize the immense amount of information available on the web.

❧ The growth of the Internet has far exceeded other forms of communication. It took 38 years for radio to reach 50 million users, 13 years for TV, and only 5 years for the Internet.

❧ Asia has the highest number of Internet users with 3,776,181,949 signing on by 2008.

I

Ivory

꙳ Ivory carvings were produced in ancient Egypt between 4,000 and 3,200 BC. Civilization in ancient Egypt was highly religious and this was reflected in the subject matters of their carvings, which generally depicted gods and goddesses.

꙳ Prior to the use of plastics, ivory was used for billiard balls, piano keys, Scottish bagpipes, and buttons.

꙳ According to wildlife conservation groups, poachers in Africa are killing more elephants today than they have anytime in the past two decades. In 2006, an estimated 23,000 elephants were killed illegally so that their ivory could be sold on the black market.

꙳ A species of hard nut is gaining popularity as an alternative to ivory, although its size limits its usability. It is called vegetable ivory, or tagua.

꙳ The narwhal is a toothed whale closely related to the all-white beluga and has a single tusk that ranges between 7 ft to 10 ft long. An exclusively Arctic species, it is hunted only in Canada and Greenland, where 300 and 500 animals are taken annually by native people. The sale of narwhal ivory is still legal, although the trade has to be monitored.

Jalapeño

🌶 Jalapeños can be sold canned, sliced, and pickled and are commonly added to products—such as sausage, cheese, and jelly—during processing. Pace Foods uses 22 million pounds a year, more fresh jalapeños than anyone else in the country.

🌶 Hot and spicy! Texas uses its two official peppers, the jalapeño and the chiltepin, in their official dish: chili.

🌶 Jalapeño pepper jelly originated in Lake Jackson, TX, and was first marketed commercially in 1978.

🌶 The jalapeño was the first pepper to be taken into space.

🌶 Dried and smoked jalapeños are chipotles, generally known in a class of their own.

🌶 The jalapeño pepper was named after the town of Jalapa in Mexico, though it is no longer commercially grown there.

J

James Bond, 007

❧ Actress Eunice Gayson, who played Sylvia Trench in the opening sequence of *Dr. No*, once stated that she was instructed to take Sean Connery out for a drink to help him relax because he was flubbing up his famous line "The name's Bond. James Bond." He accidentally kept giving his own name.

❧ *Casino Royale* is the first Bond film not to feature a female dancing silhouette in the opening titles.

❧ Author Ian Fleming wrote one Bond novel a year from 1952 (*Casino Royale*) to his death in 1964. All were written in Jamaica, where Fleming vacationed. He also wrote a story for his young son called *Chitty Chitty Bang Bang: The Magical Car*.

❧ James Bond wasn't a successful book series in America until JFK included *From Russia With Love* on a list of his favorite books in 1961.

❧ Roger Moore was the oldest Bond actor at 58.

❧ Shaken, not stirred...and often. In the films up to *Casino Royale*, Bond has a total of 114 drinks, or one every 24.3 minutes.

❧ Since the first book in 1962, Bond has killed over 150 men and slept with 44 women...¾ of whom have attempted to kill him.

Japan

❧ Japan is unrivalled when it comes to bizarre museums. The variety includes museums dedicated strictly to parasites, kites, laundromats, sand, buttons, and lighters. It's nice to finally see that sand is getting the respect it deserves.

❧ The Japanese are renowned for their longevity. There are an estimated 20,000 Japanese who are 100 years old or older living in Japan. Some attribute this to a low-calorie and cholesterol-free diet.

❧ Five couples get married each year at Tokyo's Sanrio theme park, Puroland. The Sanrio Company has a host of branded characters, but they are best known for Hello Kitty.

❧ Sociologists recognize that Hello Kitty has helped propel a cultural shift in Japan during the past generation, resulting in greater spending and relaxation.

❧ Japan boasts more than 30,000 sushi restaurants yet a sweeping majority refuse to hire women. Women are considered to have a higher body temperature and other physiological differences that may affect their preparations of something as delicate as sushi.

❧ The Japanese word *kimono* translates literally as "thing to wear."

❧ The sleeve length of a kimono can indicate a woman's marital status. Married and older women usually wear a short-sleeved kimono. Unmarried, young women wear a long-sleeved kimono, called a "furisode."

Jaws

~❧ Once during pre-production, director Steven Spielberg, along with his friends Martin Scorsese, George Lucas, and John Milius, visited the effects shop where the shark was being constructed. Lucas stuck his head in the shark's mouth to see how it operated and pranksters Milius and Spielberg snuck to the controls and made the jaw clamp shut on Lucas's head.

~❧ Charlton Heston was considered for the role of Chief Brody while Jeff Bridges, Timothy Bottoms, Jon Voight, and Jan-Michael Vincent were considered for the role of Hooper.

~❧ Steven Spielberg named the shark "Bruce" after his lawyer.

~❧ In addition to "Bruce," Steven Spielberg also called the shark "the great white turd" when he really got frustrated with the troublesome animatronic fish.

~❧ In a biography, Steven Spielberg revealed Robert Duvall's encouragement to make the film. In exchange, Spielberg offered the role of Brody to Duvall but he turned it down, fearing that it may make him too famous.

~❧ As the shoot schedule spiraled from 55 days to 159, and budgets escalated, crew members began calling the film "Flaws."

~❧ *Jaws* single-handedly caused a downturn in the package beach holiday trade.

Jell-O®

🍂 In 1897, Pearle Wait, a carpenter in LeRoy, NY was concocting a cough remedy and laxative tea in his home. He experimented with gelatin and developed a fruit-flavored dessert, which his wife, May, named Jell-O®. Without the experience and know-how to market the product, he sold his formula to a fellow townsman for the sum of $450 in 1899.

🍂 There's always time for Jell-O®...the people of Salt Lake City consume more lime-favored gelatin than any other city in the U.S. By January 2001, the Utah Senate declared Jell-O® gelatin the "Official State Snack" of Utah, in an effort to recognize the popularity of the wiggly treat in the state.

🍂 Bill Cosby has been a spokesman for Jell-O® since 1974.

🍂 On March 7, 1993, technicians at St. Jerome hospital in Batavia tested a bowl of lime Jell-O® with an EEG machine and confirmed the earlier testing by Dr. Adrian Upton that a bowl of Jell-O® has brain waves identical to those of adult men and women.

🍂 During the first quarter of the 20th century, new immigrants entering Ellis Island in New York City were served Jell-O® as a "Welcome to America."

🍂 There are currently 20 flavors of regular boxed Jell-O®, but in the beginning there were only four: orange, strawberry, raspberry, and lemon.

J

JENGA®

🐦 The highest JENGA® tower on record stood with 40 complete tiers and two blocks into the 41st.

🐦 The name JENGA® was derived from a Swahili word meaning "to build."

🐦 The JENGA® game is now available in well over 40 countries around the world.

🐦 British student Leslie Scott invented the game JENGA®. She spent her childhood in Africa playing with a set of locally made building blocks and brought the game back to England in the 70s. She started selling the game and took out copyright on the rules. JENGA® was promoted in the United States by Robert Grebler and was first manufactured there by Milton Bradley (now part of Hasbro) in 1987.

🐦 The wooden blocks for the JENGA® game come from alder trees. For years, alder trees were considered of little value and were cleared for use only as firewood. More recently, it has been discovered that alder could be an important source of hardwood, making it useful as building material for houses, furniture and, of course, JENGA® blocks.

Jimmy "Superfly" Snuka

🐦 His look and attire was purely Polynesian. He often wore a headband made of shells, animal-printed or floral-designed trunks, and wrestled barefoot.

🐦 His nickname "Superfly" apparently came from his acrobatic skills and moves, including his signature wrestling move, the Superfly Splash, where Snuka would leave his stunned opponent laying on the mat, and then he would climb onto a corner of the ring's ropes, stand up, and dive face down, landing on the opponent in pin position (unless the opponent revived and moved out of the way of course). He was also known for his backhand chop.

🐦 Jimmy had a year-long feud with Rowdy Roddy Piper. After a segment on "Piper's Pit" where Piper berated Jimmy by calling him a "big shot" and "monkey," Piper proceeded to smash a coconut on Jimmy's head, who had his back turned at the time. This was followed by a beating with a belt and further humiliation before the WWF cut to a commercial.

🐦 He also goes by the following names: The Big Snuka, Superfly Snuka, Jimmy Snuka, Jimmy Kealoha, Lani Kealoha, The Great Snuka, and SupaSplash.

🐦 The Superfly is currently working on a reality show which will feature him in various 9–5 jobs at places you'd never expect to see him.

J

Joan of Arc

🖎 Joan of Arc wore men's clothing between her departure from Vaucouleurs and her abjuration at Rouen. One justifiable reason she did this was for preservation of chastity—her apparel would have slowed an assailant, and men would be less likely to objectify her.

🖎 Prophecy foretold that a maid from Lorraine would save France. This prediction was well known in France during Joan's time and has been attributed to several prophets including the mythical Merlin.

🖎 Joan was twelve when she first heard a Voice from God in her father's garden. Her voices told her she must deliver her country from the invading English.

🖎 Joan carried a banner with a picture of God and the words "Jesus Mary" written on it.

🖎 Joan predicted she would be wounded in the exact manner that it occurred in several sources, including a letter written fifteen days before the event. She was wounded by an arrow above her breast during an attack upon the fort Les Tourelles.

🖎 Joan of Arc was threatened with torture unless she denied her Voices. She was burned to death on May 30, 1431. Her last words were: "Jesus, Jesus, Jesus!"

Kangaroos

❧ A male kangaroo is also called an old man.

❧ One of the largest kangaroo species—the Western Grey Kangaroos—are known as stinkers because mature males have a distinctive curry-like odor.

❧ More than a hop and a skip, a kangaroo can jump 45 ft.

❧ Unlike other four-legged mammals, kangaroos cannot walk backwards.

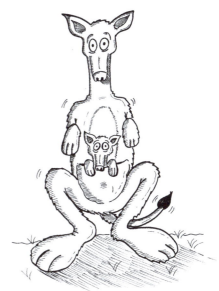

❧ A mother kangaroo can produce two different types of milk to feed two different babies (joeys) simultaneously: a joey that has emerged from the pouch but is still nursing as well as a newborn.

K

Kellogg's® Cornflakes

 John Harvey Kellogg (February 26, 1852–December 14, 1943) was an American medical doctor in Battle Creek, MI. He ran a sanitarium using holistic methods and paid particular attention to nutrition, enemas, and exercise. Kellogg was an advocate of vegetarianism and is best known for the invention of the corn flakes breakfast cereal with his brother, Will Keith Kellogg. The cereal was originally invented for a patient with bad teeth.

In the early days, Will Keith Kellogg would actually sign his name to each box of cereal, to guarantee the quality and authenticity of the article. The Kellogg's logo used today was derived from the original signature: "W.K. Kellogg."

K

Corn flake cereals are made from white corn grits.

In 1907, one of the ad campaigns for Kellogg's® Corn Flakes offered a free box of cereal to every woman who would wink at her grocer.

One serving cup of Kellogg's® Cornflakes has 101 calories.

Kennedy, John F.

❧ John Kennedy was 6 ft 1 in tall, and he kept his weight at 175 lbs.

❧ He was known to change his clothes twice a day and often wore as many as four different shirts on a single day. He particularly disliked button-down collars, and ordered the members of his staff to stop wearing them.

❧ John Kennedy was the youngest elected president at 43 years old as well as the youngest to die in office, at the age of 46.

❧ He is the only president to have won a Pulitzer Prize for his collective biography, *Profiles in Courage.*

❧ Although strictly coincidental, JFK and Abraham shared some unusual history. Lincoln was elected in 1860, Kennedy in 1960; Lincoln's secretary was named Kennedy, Kennedy's was named Lincoln; both men were assassinated; and both men were succeeded by their vice presidents, both of whom were named Johnson.

❧ Kennedy always had a black alligator briefcase that he carried around even while at Camp David or Cape Cod.

❧ His favorite foods were ice cream with hot fudge and New England Fish Chowder.

K

Kentucky

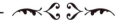

❧ Kentucky blues…Many residents of Troublesome Creek, Kentucky have blue skin due to a recessive blue gene brought over by a man in the early 19th century from France.

❧ The word Kentucky is based on the Cherokee Indian word *Ken-tah-ten*, meaning "land of tomorrow."

❧ In 1998, the town of Rabbit Hash in Kentucky elected a dog named Goofy as their mayor. The small town charged $1 per vote and proceeds went to restore a local church.

❧ Duncan Hines, the traveling salesman-cum-food-critic was born in Bowling Green, Kentucky in 1880. In 1953, Hines sold the right to use his name and the title of his book to Roy H. Park to form Hines-Park Foods, which licensed the name to a number of food-related businesses. The cake mix license was sold to Nebraska Consolidated Mills in Omaha, which developed and sold the first Duncan Hines cake mix.

❧ Garrett Augustus Morgan was an African-American businessman and inventor born in Paris, Kentucky in 1877. Among his inventions was a zigzag stitching attachment for manually operated sewing machines, and he also founded a company that made personal grooming products, such as hair dying ointments and the curved-tooth pressing comb. His greatest contribution to society was his invention of an early three-colored traffic signal.

Ketchup

❧ The word "ketchup" comes from the Chinese *ketsiap*, which is entirely unlike the tomato-based condiment we know today, but rather a sauce made from pickled fish. When English and Dutch sailors traveled to the Far East in the 17th century, they discovered the sauce and brought some back with them. Homemade versions became a hit almost instantly. By the early 1700s, someone thought to add tomatoes to the ketsiap and by the mid-19th century, Teresa Heinz Kerry's ancestors began selling a thin, salty version called "tomato ketchup" in 1876. It became so popular that they dropped the "tomato."

❧ Henry Heinz chose the company's famous slogan "57 Varieties" in 1892 after he saw an advertisement for "21 varieties of shoes" in an elevated train car in New York.

❧ In India, Heinz Ketchup is available in glass bottles with two varieties. One is the standard Heinz Ketchup, and the other is an alternative, which does not contain any traces of garlic or onion. The latter version appeals to the many Indians who refrain from eating garlic and onion for religious and cultural reasons.

❧ Not only does it taste great with French fries, it is ideal for restoring the glow to copper pots and pans. The acid in ketchup removes tarnish and brings out the shine.

K

❧ Early in the administration of Ronald Reagan, the United States Department of Agriculture proposed to reclassify ketchup from a condiment to a vegetable, allowing public schools to cut out a serving of vegetables from hot food lunch programs. The proposal was met with outrage and billed as "ketchupgate."

Kilt

🍃 Each kilt is made of about eight yards of material.

🍃 An average worsted wool kilt weighs between 4.5 to 5 lb.

🍃 A handmade kilt requires a total of 15 hours of labor to complete.

🍃 There are more than 4,000 recognized tartan designs on record to date.

🍃 The most popular tartans are the Stewart tartans, Black Watch, Dress Gordon, and the Flower of Scotland.

🍃 The Falkirk tartan, which dates to around 260 AD, is the oldest tartan and was discovered in a jar of coins near Falkirk.

🍃 Kilts are not native to Scotland. They originated in France.

K

King Jr., Martin Luther

🕊 In the wake of the "I Have a Dream" speech and march, King was saluted as "Man of the Year" by *Time* magazine for 1963, and in 1964, he was the youngest person ever awarded the Nobel Peace Prize.

🕊 King's non-violent doctrines were greatly steered by the teachings of Gandhi.

🕊 Because of his intelligence, he was placed into the first grade at the age of five, but was expelled when his teacher discovered his age. By fifteen, King had already graduated from high school.

🕊 By January 17, 2000, Martin Luther King Jr. Day was officially observed in all fifty U.S. states.

🕊 King received numerous awards and accolades, including at least fifty honorary degrees from various colleges and universities in the U.S. and abroad.

K

King, Stephen

🕊 Stephen King's first best-selling novel, *Carrie*, was tossed in the trash because he was unhappy with it. It was his wife, Tabitha King, who convinced him that she loved the novel and that it was worth keeping.

🕊 Stephen King—along with Dave Barry, Amy Tan, and many others—is a member of the band, The Rock Bottom Remainders.

🕊 Derry and Castle Rock, ME, only exist in Stephen King's stories. If they were actual towns, Derry would be located a few miles west of Bangor, while Bangor would be situated south of the city of Mexico in the Oxford District of Maine.

🕊 Many of King's earlier books were written in an alcohol- and drug-induced haze. He is a recovering coke addict, alcoholic, and smoker who credits his wife in helping him quit.

🕊 Stephen King has often expressed his disappointment with Stanley Kubrick's adaptation of *The Shining*. "There's a lot to like about it. But it's a great big beautiful Cadillac with no motor inside, you can sit in it and you can enjoy the smell of the leather upholstery—the only thing you can't do is drive it anywhere."

K

Kiss

- The scientific name for kissing is philematology.

- Kissing stimulates 29 muscles and chemicals causing relaxation.

- The average person burns 26 calories in a one-minute kiss.

- This average person also spends two weeks of his/her life kissing.

- In 1562, kissing was banned in Naples, Italy, under punishment of death. The law lasted for approximately one day before the local nobleman was forced to rescind it because so many in his own palace were violating the law.

- In Russia, the highest sign of recognition was a kiss from the Tsar.

- The popular photograph "The Kiss at L'Hôtel de Ville" shot by photographer Robert Doisneau became a bestseller through poster and postcard reprints since1896. Dozens of people claimed to the be the kissers in the scene, including Denis and Jean-Louis Lavergne who sued Doisneau for $100,000 and lost their case when it was determined that the kiss was between two professional models.

Knickers

🍂 In Australian and British usage the term is often used in the expressions "Don't get your knickers in a twist" and "Don't get your knickers in a knot." The U.S. equivalent is "don't get your panties in a bunch."

🍂 In India, boys or men's shorts are called knickers; they are not a term exclusively used for women's underwear.

🍂 French Knickers is a term predominantly used in the UK to describe a type of underwear worn from the hip. They cover the hip, part of the upper thigh and part of the buttocks. They are regarded as more comfortable and sexier than thongs.

🍂 Japanese inventor Katsu Kkaturgoru, whose greatest fear was drowning, invented inflatable underwear. The garment once accidentally inflated to 30 times its original size in a crowded subway.

🍂 Astronauts wear underwear lined with tubes of water to keep cool.

K

Knight Rider

- The original *Knight Rider* series spun off a second NBC series in the 80s called *Code of Vengeance*.

- In South America, the show aired as *El Auto Fantastico* (The Fantastic Car).

- KITT, the Knight Industries Two-Thousand, was a customized 1982 Pontiac Trans-Am.

- Pontiac, who supplied the Trans Am for the series, found itself swamped with customer requests for black Firebird Trans Ams with T-tops, tan interiors, and red lights on the front bumper, just like the show's car.

K

- When dodging pursuers, K.I.T.T. rotated its license plate from KNIGHT to KNI 667. Stealth.

- David Hasselhoff once described his acting as "a little more difficult than if you had a regularly well-written script—like, if I was going to be in, say, *Reservoir Dogs,* or *The Godfather,* or *Dances with Wolves* or *Lawrence of Arabia* or *ER.* I had to talk to a car."

Languages

◆ Aramaic, the ancient language spoken by Jesus Christ, today is spoken in only three remote villages near Damascus, Syria.

◆ English contains the most words of any language, including 455,000 active words and 700,000 dead ones.

◆ Reading an average Chinese newspaper requires the knowledge of 7,000 Chinese characters.

◆ Papua New Guinea has 820 living languages, making it the country with the most languages spoken.

◆ French was the official language of England for over 600 years.

◆ The longest word in the English language, according to the Oxford English Dictionary, is *pneumonoultramicroscopicsilicovolcanokoniosis*. The only other word with the same amount of letters is *pneumonoultra-microscopicsilicovolcanoconioses*, its plural.

L

Laws

- In Maine, it was against the law for a police officer to arrest a dead man.

- In Houston, TX, it was made illegal to make a noise while moving boxes.

- In Sioux Falls, SD, all hotels in the city must make sure that every room has two twin beds, which should be a minimum of at least two ft apart from each other.

- In North Carolina, singing off key in public could get you arrested.

- A law in Texas states that it is illegal to sell one's eye—right or left.

L

Leather

🐦 Most consumers mistakenly assume that leather is merely a by-product of the meat industry, and that buying leather clothing does not increase the number of animals slaughtered. They are actually two separate industries.

🐦 Ostrich leather is commonly available in New Zealand. It has a unique feather quill pattern, which provides added strength and durability—7 times stronger than cowhide.

🐦 Your leather shoes could save you in certain predicaments. A person who is lost or starving can eat leather and obtain enough nourishment to sustain life for a short time.

🐦 Though unusual, bullfrog skins can be used to make a diverse array of products. They are smooth, available in an assortment of colors, and have patterns/styles unlike other leathers.

🐦 Stingray, also known as "Shagreen," often falls short in the limelight of leathers, but it is 25 times more durable than cowhide leather and has a unique supple texture. It can be textured to be bumpy or flat and can also be painted in any color. Under no threat of extinction, this fish provides a useful resource to many regions throughout Southeast Asia. They can be made into handbags, shoes, boots, and wallets.

L

Lightning

- Rubber shoes will do nothing to protect one from lightning.

- Talking on the telephone is the leading cause of lightning injuries inside the home.

- Standing under a tall tree is one of the most dangerous places to take shelter.

- Lightning can reach over five miles in length, raise the temperature of the air by as much as 50,000°F, and can contain a hundred million electrical volts.

- Thunderstruck! Lightning is not confined just to thunderstorms. It has been visible in volcanic eruptions, extremely intense forest fires, surface nuclear detonations, heavy snowstorms, and in large hurricanes.

- In the U.S., the odds of being struck by lightning in any one year is 1 in 700,000. The odds of being struck in a lifetime is 1 in 3,000. About 400 people survive lightning strikes in the U.S. each year.

- Red hot…the recent discovery of Red Sprite lightning has fascinated both scientists and the general public. This new type of lightning is discharged very high in the atmosphere, a 40-mile span between the tops of severe storm clouds to the lower ionosphere "D" layer. They are predominantly red and last for a fraction of a second. Scientists are uncertain of the cause.

L

Lincoln, Abraham

🐦 Lincoln was a mill manager, postmaster and lawyer before becoming president.

🐦 Lincoln had a notoriously cluttered law office, which became a constant source of irritation to his partner, William Herndon. On his desk, Lincoln kept one envelope marked "When you can't find it anywhere else, look into this."

🐦 After the death of his son Willie, Lincoln's wife convinced him to participate in several séances held in the White House. The President was fascinated by psychic phenomena and wanted to communicate with his dead son.

🐦 Lincoln was 6 ft 4 in and the first president to have a beard while in office.

🐦 Lincoln had a cat named "Bob," a turkey named "Jack," and a dog named "Jib."

🐦 Lincoln's favorite sport was wrestling…hands down.

🐦 Abraham Lincoln was the only president to be awarded a patent—for a device that buoyed life vessels over shoals without discharging their cargo.

L

Locusts

🐛 There are several edible species of locusts that are important food sources in some areas, especially Africa. They can be grilled, roasted, or boiled, and also ground to a paste.

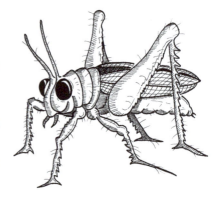

🐛 The largest swarm of locusts recorded was in 1874 in the state of California. Entomologists recorded a swarm covering 198,000 square miles with an estimated 12.5 trillion locusts.

L

🐛 A large swarm may eat up to 80,000 tons of grain and other vegetation in a day.

🐛 Locusts can jump 2.3 ft, which is equivalent to a human jumping 60 ft.

🐛 Locusts and grasshoppers have a similar look and habits, but locusts have shorter antennae and "sing" by rubbing their rear feet from elytra (the outer tough pair of wings), whereas grasshoppers "sing" by rubbing the elytra between them.

🐛 The locust is the first insect ever drawn by humans. A drawing was found in a 10,000-year-old bison (wisent) bone located in a French cave.

Louvre

🐦 The Louvre was not supposed to be a museum; it was intended to be a place for Henry VI's drawings and paintings.

🐦 Three almost invisible drawings were discovered on the back of Leonardo da Vinci's *Virgin and Child With Saint Anne*, currently found in the Louvre.

🐦 The Musée du Louvre houses 35,000 works of art drawn from eight departments, displayed in over 60,000 square meters of exhibition space dedicated to the permanent collections.

🐦 The Mona Lisa was stolen from the Louvre Museum in Paris in broad daylight by an employee in 1911, but it was recovered two years later. The painting resides in its own room in the Louvre, protected in a climate-controlled environment and encased in bulletproof glass. Because the painting is considered priceless and cannot be insured, a room was built for it and cost the museum over seven million dollars.

L

Madonna

❧ Thunder and lightning, very, very frightening me…Madge suffers from "brontophobia," a morbid fear of thunder.

❧ In 1989, Pepsi-Cola paid Madonna $5 million for an ad she did. Unfortunately, this happened immediately after her single "Like a Prayer" caused international controversy. The ad was pulled from circulation only after airing once.

❧ Who's got spirit fingers? In contrast to the provocative tough-girl image she's nurtured over the years, Madonna was an enthusiastic cheerleader, straight A student, and helped to create a high school drama club.

❧ Madonna allegedly rejected the female lead in Prince's *Graffiti Bridge*, because the screenplay was awful. This is coming from the same woman who gave a thumbs up to *Shanghai Surprise*, *Swept Away*, *Dick Tracy*, and *Body of Evidence*. Lest we forget, she also received Razzie awards for Worst Actress on more than one occasion.

❧ Madonna's first band was called The Breakfast Club.

❧ Madonna's father is a vintner who created limited-edition Madonna wine in the Ciccone vineyards…in Michigan.

Malcolm X

🐦 "By any means necessary."—Malcolm X

🐦 Malcolm X befriended and ministered a boxer named Cassius Clay who eventually decided to convert to the Muslim religion and join the Nation of Islam. In February 1964, the boxer converted his name to Muhammad Ali.

🐦 Spike Lee's film *Malcolm X* was the first non-documentary production to be filmed in Mecca.

🐦 Malcolm's father was murdered, and his mother was committed to a mental hospital by the time he was 13.

🐦 Malcolm considered his surname "Little" a slave name and so then changed it to "X" which represented his lost tribal name.

🐦 On February 21, 1965, Malcolm X was assassinated in the Manhattan's Audubon Ballroom by three members of the Nation of Islam.

M

Marmite®

- Unilever, the same company that gives us Vaseline, Dove soap, and Hellman's Mayonnaise, also owns Marmite®.

- The spread is a sticky, dark brown paste made primarily with yeast extract and has a distinctive, salty and savory flavor. It contains five "B" vitamins, which are good for the nervous system, muscle tone, skin, eyes, liver, and hair.

- With sales topping £23.5 million, Marmite® is one of UK's premier savour spreads, conquering the meat and vegetable extract market. In 1995, it was consumed in 24.3% of households.

M

- Marmite® was included in soldier's rations for WWI and offered to prisoners of war as a dietary supplement in WWII.

- The name "Marmite" comes from a French word for an earthenware pot, in which the spread was once sold. The design of the glass jar is based on the pot and an image of it is featured on the front of bottles.

Marriage

🕊 According to the *Monogomy Myth* by Peggy Vaughan, about 60% of men and 40% of women will have an affair at some point in their marriage.

🕊 A couple gets divorced every ten to thirteen seconds.

🕊 Men in marriages are more likely to have good relationships with their children. 65% of young adults whose parents divorced had poor relationships with their fathers compared to 29% from non-divorced families.

🕊 Statistically, married men earn 10–40% more financially than single men with similar education backgrounds and job experiences.

🕊 The exchange of rings is a tradition that harkens back to ancient Roman times. The roundness of the ring is to represent eternity and the donning of the wedding bands signifies an eternal union. It was once believed that the vein of the ring finger on the left hand ran directly to the heart.

🕊 At a Hindu wedding, the bride's hands are painted with an intricate henna design, which often includes the initials of the groom. The couple is then to search for the initials on a wedding night, which is meant to encourage the bride and groom to relax and feel more at ease with one another.

McDonald's®

❧ McDonald's® fast food restaurant opened an official training school—Hamburger University—in Oak Brook, IL, in 1961. School's in McSession!

❧ McDonald's® purchases the most beef in the world.

❧ Space is probably one thing that cannot be super sized. The smallest McDonald's® restaurant is located in Ginza in Tokyo, Japan, and measures a measly 492 sq ft.

❧ The only McDonald's restaurants that do not sell beef are located in India. As an alternative, patrons can purchase an all-lamb version of the Big Mac® called the "Maharaja Mac™."

❧ Israel is one of the few countries that cooks the meat over charcoal versus frying. They also have the McKebab®: two patties with Middle Eastern seasonings and stuffed into a pita bread.

❧ Our McMates from Down Under can enjoy a cheeseburger with beetroot called a "McOz®."

❧ "McKroket®" is a semi-crispy shelled beefy patty with a creamy mayo-based sauce served in Holland.

Mercury

🐦 Mercury, also known as quicksilver, has a silvery color, and reflective metallic nature.

🐦 Heavy metal...mercury is the heaviest known liquid element, and it's so dense that bricks, cannonballs, lumps of lead, and iron will float in it.

🐦 Mercury is unlike other liquids in the fact that it is not actually "wet" and it can be held in the hand. However, this is strongly discouraged, as the mercury is toxic and will soak into the skin.

🐦 The main source of human exposure to mercury is through fish, which store the element in their muscles. When consumed by humans, it can cause liver, kidney, and skin damage.

🐦 Alchemists loved working with mercury as it was believed that all life was formed from the element and when it hardened, it turned to gold.

🐦 The term Mad Hatter did not derive from the popular children's book, *Alice's Adventures in Wonderland*. Milliners were called Mad Hatters in the 18th and 19th century due to their use of mercury to remove animal fur from the materials. As a result, the extensive work with mercury and the exposure to its vapours caused serious physical and mental damage.

M

Mexico

* Sangrita is a chaser made traditionally with tomatoes, orange juice, fresh limejuice, onions, salt and hot chili peppers. Originating in the state of Jalisco, it was designed to quench the heat of homemade tequila and thus began a longstanding Mexican tradition. Typically, sangrita allows one to alternate between sipping premium tequila and the elixir.

* A Mexican jumping bean is a novelty item that has been around for decades. The jumping beans are actually a type of seed in which the egg of a small moth has been laid and the moth's larva causes the "jump."

* Fowl play? Turkeys originated in Mexico. The wild turkey was domesticated by pre-Columbian Indians way before the Spanish conquistadors arrived.

* The world's smallest volcano is located in the city of Puebla, Mexico. Standing at a mere 43 ft tall, the Cuexcomate is considered inactive now and has a spiralled staircase inside just for tourists. This brings up the age-old question, does size *really* matter?

* Mexico City, the largest city in the world, is built over the ruins of the ancient Aztec city, Tenochtitlán. The city is actually built over a water reserve and so to provide water for the millions of citizens, the city is sinking at a rate of 6–8 in each year.

Michelin Man

● Michelin's company mascot Bibendum, also known as "Bib the Michelin Man," was introduced to the world in 1898 and hails as one of the world's oldest trademarks.

● In Spain, the term Michelín is now used to apply to folds of fatty skin around the waist.

● Cayce Pollard—the protagonist of William Gibson's 2003 book *Pattern Recognition*—has a phobia of the Michelin Man.

● Michelin Tire Baby Syndrome is a disease of babies born with multiple, symmetric, circumferential skin creases, or bands, on the forearms, lower legs, and neck. The creases eventually disappear as the child grows older.

● Bibendum, the Michelin Man, is what some might describe as the strong silent type…especially since he does not actually speak.

M

Money

 Between 9000 and 6000 BC, without any other means of monetary units, primitive people used cattle as money.

 Because of shortages of suitable metal for coinage, the Chinese were the first people to issue paper money in 700 AD. By 1455, the paper money was withdrawn in an effort to curb inflation.

 Between 1642–51, during the English Civil Wars, goldsmiths offered their safes as secure places for deposits of valuable goods. Depositors would provide written instructions to a goldsmith to pay money to a third person, with the deposited article as valued collateral. These written instructions are the originations of the modern check.

 The word "dollar" comes from the Czech currency *thaler* which was first minted in 1519. *Thaler* (phonetically "tarler") was mispronounced in England as "dollar."

 The U.S. Federal Government began printing paper currency in 1861. When they were released in 1862, the bills had to be individually signed by hand by six people who were hired to work in the attic of the Treasury building to sign, sort, and seal the notes.

M

Monopoly®

🐦 The official mascot of Monopoly®, originally known as Rich Uncle Pennybags, was renamed Mr. Monopoly in 1998.

🐦 Every Monopoly® set includes $15,140 of play money.

🐦 During WWII, maps, compasses, and money were smuggled to prisoners of war through Monopoly® sets.

🐦 In the 1970s, Hasbro created a Monopoly® edition in Braille for the blind, but it was never released to the general public.

🐦 In Cuba, the game once had a solid following until Fidel Castro took reign over the country and ordered all known sets destroyed.

🐦 According to *The Guinness Book of World Records*, the most expensive Monopoly set is made of 23-carat gold with the houses and hotels decorated in rubies and sapphires. Its value? A whopping $2,000,000.

M

Mozart, Wolfgang Amadeus

- Mozart was a Freemason and admitted to the lodge *Zur Wohltätigkeit* ("Beneficence"). He was an avid participant and took his role seriously by attending many meetings and composing Masonic music.

- Mozart was composing and performing music by the age of six.

- Mozart produced over 600 musical compositions before he passed away on December 5, 1791. He was only 35.

- Mozart had a slightly hooked nose, possibly as a result of being punched in the face as a child by a fellow composer.

- Valerie Bertinelli and Eddie Van Halen named their son, Wolfgang Van Halen, after the composer.

Mummies

When examined at the Wayne State University School of Medicine in Detroit, MI, a 2,700-year-old Egyptian mummy was found to still have red-painted fingernails.

In 1994, archaeologists in Zanjan, Iran, discovered a perfectly preserved body of a man who was buried in a salt quarry, 2,600 years prior.

The 700-year-old corpse of a Chinese man found in a tomb in the Kiangsu province of Eastern China, was so well preserved that its joints could be moved and its skin and hair remained in good condition.

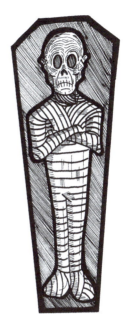

The mummy museum in Guanajuanto, Mexico, is home to 108 forgotten corpses. They're so intact that visitors can usually determine the cause of death just by looking—whether it be noose marks around the neck or a fatal tumor. The most disturbing of all is the body of a woman whom curators only know as "Ignaciam." With her raised arms and expression of horror, the curators believe that she was buried alive.

M

Museums

✦ The Nut Museum in Old Lyme, CT, exhibits nuts from all over the world—including a 35 lb double coconut.

✦ Chincoteague, VA, boasts a museum devoted to oysters.

✦ Until recently, there was a pretzel museum in Philadelphia, but the idea was probably too twisted.

✦ The Spam Museum in Austin, MN, features nearly 5,000 cans of SPAM. One of the highlights includes a scale model of a SPAM plant where visitors can pretend to produce one of America's favorite meat bi-products. The museum also organizes a SPAM Museum Jam.

M

✦ The College of Physicians of Philadelphia's Mütter Museum serves as a popular spot for anyone interested in the grotesque. One can find the world's largest colon, an OB-GYN instrument collection, thousands of fluid-preserved anatomical and pathological specimens, and a large wall dedicated entirely to swallowed objects.

Mushrooms

❧ Officially known as *Armillaria ostoyae*, the honey mushroom is the largest living organism in the world. Located in the Malheur National Forest in eastern Oregon, it spans 3.5 miles across and covers approximately 2,200 acres. Experts estimate the fungi to be at least 2,400 years old, but it could be 7,200 years old.

❧ Some mushrooms can produce cancer-fighting compounds. A Japanese scientist discovered that a particular community had unusually low cancer rates and many of them grew and ate Enokitake mushrooms.

M

❧ In 2004, the world's most expensive truffle at the time was sold for $50,000 to clients of a fashionable Italian restaurant in London. However, the unimaginable happened. The 850g of white truffle went bad, putrefied, and became inedible. The truffle was eventually buried with hopes that it would regenerate and produce another truffle.

❧ Mushrooms can be used as a dye by boiling wild mushrooms and soaking cloth in the resulting broth.

❧ Mushrooms have also been known as the "vegetarians' beefsteak" because no other vegetable comes close to having the taste and texture of meat.

NASA

 So you want to be an astronaut, huh? NASA's application process is thorough, and the competition is fierce. Minimum requirements include a bachelor's degree in engineering, science, or mathematics from an accredited institution. In addition, applicants should have substantial related experience and pilot astronauts must have at least 1,000 hours of experience in jet aircraft. Space cases need not apply.

N

 For 2009, NASA's projected budget for the fiscal year was over $7.6 billion, only 1.8% more than their 2008 projection.

 Though Eisenhower was the president who signed the papers to create NASA, only Kennedy and Johnson have Space Centers named after them.

 Alan Shepard is the only person to hit a golf ball on the moon. He played with a Wilson six-iron head attached to a lunar sample scoop handle. One giant leap...FORE!

 The United States spent approximately $40 billion to get a spacecraft and astronauts onto the moon.

Native Americans

🍂 Native Americans (American Indians) make up less than 1% of the total U.S. population, but they represent half the languages and cultures in the nation.

🍂 Chewing gum and popcorn were both developed by Native Americans.

🍂 The Native Indians were "animists" who believed that every animal, plant, and object in nature contained a spirit to be propitiated or feared. Some of these—including the sun, the buffalo, the peyote plant, the eagle and the rattlesnake—were more powerful or more frequently helpful than others, but there was nothing mightier than the "Great Spirit," which was frequently represented.

🍂 A general belief is that all American Indians lived in tipis but this isn't true. In reality, only the Plains Indians lived in them. The Hope Indians lived in mud huts and the Anasazi Indians lived in cliff houses to prevent attacks from enemies.

🍂 It's common knowledge that many words in the American language are derived from other languages. The Native Indians gave us words such as "squash," "raccoon," and "bayou." Suffering succotash—and that one as well!

N

Neon

❧ The word neon is derived from the Greek word *neos* meaning "new."

❧ Neon is most commonly used for lights, signs, high-voltage indicators, gas discharge lightning arrestors, and television tubes.

❧ Neon is produced by liquefying air under high pressure at temperatures of −200°C. It takes 88,000 lbs of liquefied air to create one pound of neon.

❧ Although neon is the fourth most abundant element in the universe, only 0.0018% of the earth's atmosphere is neon.

N ❧ Neon signs are simply glass tubes filled with neon gas. Blue neon has a few drops of mercury added to it.

Nettle

❧ Nettle was used by the German army in WWI to make uniforms following a shortage of cotton. At the time, uniforms were found to contain 85% nettle fiber.

❧ High in fiber, the older leaves of nettle can be used as a laxative. However, readers should always consult medical experts before consuming it.

❧ Back in its heyday, nettle was used for contraception as a prescribed gypsy remedy. The man had to line his socks with nettle leaves and wear them for 24 hours prior to intercourse.

❧ Competitors travel as far as Belgium, New York, and Australia to participate in the World Nettle Eating Championships held each year at the Bottle Inn in Dorset, England. The challengers have one hour to eat as many stinging nettles as possible on the condition that they do not bring their own nettles or use any mouth-numbing substances...though a swig of beer has been deemed acceptable.

❧ The leaves of stinging nettle have been used in Europe to treat urinary tract infections. The plant acts as a mild diuretic when consumed with a substantial amount of liquid, and can be used to flush out bladder inflammation and prevent kidney stones.

N

New York City

❧ When *The New York Times* was bought by Adolph Ochs in 1896, it was soon given its notorious slogan "All the News That's Fit to Print" was a jab at rivals such as *New York World* and the *New York Journal American,* which were known for "yellow journalism" (a type of journalism which focuses on sensational headlines rather than legitimate news to sell papers).

❧ In 1904, *The New York Times* moved to 42nd street, giving the surrounding area the name, Times Square.

❧ One of the towers of the Brooklyn Bridge is set on sand instead of bedrock.

N ❧ New York City was the capital of the United States in the 1780s before the capital was moved to Philadelphia, and then Washington D.C.

❧ 36% of the current population of New York City is comprised of people who were born outside the United States.

❧ The New York subway system is the largest mass transit system in the world with 468 stations and 842 miles (1355 km) of track. It also runs 24 hours a day, 7 days a week.

❧ Street performers must audition to perform in the NYC Subway system. Some have even played at Carnegie Hall.

Nobel Prize

❧ A French newspaper mistakenly ran an obituary for Alfred Nobel, the inventor of dynamite. The premature obituary reflected none of his interests in humanity, love of people, or generosity. This led him to create the Nobel Prizes that awarded individuals who did the most to advance peace, literature, and the sciences.

❧ Tolstoy was rejected for an award in the first year of the Nobel Prize. He was nominated the following year but was rejected again.

❧ In 1997, Robert E. Lucas won the Nobel Prize in economics for his theory of "rational expectations." Unfortunately, he had to split the $1 million prize winnings with his ex-wife, whose divorce lawyer had included a contractual clause to cover such a possibility.

❧ Jean Paul Sartre refused the prize ($53,000) for literature in 1964.

❧ All in the family! Marie Curie won two Nobel Prizes: one for physics (which she shared with her husband) and one for chemistry. Her daughter, Irene, also won a Nobel Prize in chemistry in 1935.

❧ The Ig Nobel Prize is a parody which annually honors research "that cannot or should not be repeated." In nutrition, Massimiliano Zampini and Charles Spence won the award for their research showing that food actually tastes better if it sounds crunchier. Geoffrey Miller, Joshua Tyber, and Brent Jordan won the award in economics for their studies which concluded that the fertility cycle of a lap dancer affects her tip-earning potential.

North Pole

 Pole position! There are actually two North Poles. The north terrestrial pole is the fixed point that, along with the south terrestrial pole, forms Earth's spinning axis. The north magnetic pole is the position where a compass needle points and moves day by day—it can shift between 6–25 miles each year.

 No land exists under the ice of the North Pole. The Arctic ice cap is a floating pack of ice between 6.5 to 10 ft thick. During the winter, the ice pack can grow to the size of the U.S.; while in the summer, half of it melts.

N

 The tiny bird called the Arctic tern has the longest migration by travelling from pole to pole. The annual journey is approximately 21,750 miles.

 The North Pole is warmest in July, when the temperature rises to 32°F and coldest in February when temperatures drop to −31°F, not including the wind chills which make it much worse.

 Every year, about 100,000 letters addressed to "Santa Claus, North Pole," find their way to Alaska, which has a town named North Pole.

Obama, Barack

🕊 "They're going to try to say that I'm a risky guy. They're going to try to say, well, you know, he's got a funny name, and he doesn't look like all the presidents on the dollar bills and the $5 bills."—Barack Obama

🕊 As an adult, Obama admitted at the 2008 Civil Forum on the Presidency that he had used marijuana, cocaine, and alcohol when in high school, which he described as his greatest moral failure.

🕊 He is a cigarette smoker, though he's been trying to quit with nicorette gum.

🕊 His childhood nickname was "Barry," though his high school friends would more likely know him as "O'Bomber" for his basketball feats.

🕊 Working at a local Baskin-Robbins as a teenager helped to cement adult Obama's distaste for ice cream.

🕊 Love at first sight…on their first date, he took wife Michelle to see Spike Lee's movie, *Do the Right Thing*.

🕊 He has won Grammy Awards for Best Spoken Word Albums for the abridged audiobook versions of his books; *Dreams from My Father* (Feb 2006) and *The Audacity of Hope* (Feb 2008).

🕊 Rearranging the letters in "Barack Hussein Obama, Jr." can create the anagram "Job: I am a Bush ransacker."

O

Octopus

🐙 *Sannakji* is live octopus that has been cut into small pieces and seasoned with sesame and sesame oil. It's a Korean delicacy, but eat it at your own risk. As the tentacles are still squirming, the cups of the arm pieces are still active and can stick to the mouth and throat while eating.

🐙 If an octopus is endangered and has no other alternative, it can lose an arm to escape a predator's clutches and re-grow it without any permanent damage.

🐙 An octopus has an average life span of one year and is considered the most advanced and complex species of the mollusk family.

🐙 The octopus has many muscles in its arms and mantle. In fact, the biggest difference between the muscles of an octopus and a human being is that we have bones attached to our muscles and they do not.

🐙 Heart to heart…to heart? The octopus has three hearts…one for each gill.

🐙 An octopus will change its color to red or white when it is stressed or under threat. If that has not deterred its predator, the octopus will release a cloud of ink to escape.

Olympics

❧ The modern Olympics first took place in Athens, Greece in 1896, but the father of the Olympic games was a Dr. William Penny Brookes who staged his version in a small English town called Much Wenlock. His idea was to revive the Olympic idea so that it would have a global impact, and his Wenlock Olympic games lead to the Olympics as we know it.

❧ In ancient times, females were forbidden from watching the games and if caught doing so, could be put to death. Only free males were allowed to participate in the games.

❧ The Olympic Flame represents the fire stolen from the Greek God Zeus. Months before the opening of the games, the torch is lit at the ancient site in Olympia. Eleven "priestesses" perform a ceremony in which the torch is lit by a parabolic mirror which condense the sun's rays.

O

❧ The marathon is officially 26 miles with the exception of the games in 1908. Organizers added an additional 385 yards in order for the royal family to have a better view of the finish line. It must've been a running joke with the officials.

❧ The five rings of the Olympics represent the five significant continents and linked to symbolize the friendship to be gained from these international competitions. The ring colors—blue, yellow, black, green, and red—were chosen because at least one of the colors appears on the flag of every country in the world.

Orchid

🌱 Orchids are the largest family of flowering plants with more than 100,000 kinds of purebreds and hybrids. In addition, approximately 800 new species are added each year.

🌱 In 2004, Britain's rarest orchid was stolen from the grounds of a Lancashire golf club. The 80-year-old, purple and yellow Lady's Slipper orchid—estimated to be worth £2,000 on the black market—was dug up from a flowerbed and never recovered.

🌱 The rare ghost orchid was made famous in the non-fiction book *The Orchid Thief* and the fictional movie *Adaptation*, but it has been discovered to grow high in an old cypress tree in a southwest Florida nature preserve. It can only be seen with binoculars and good lighting.

🌱 The *Grammatophyllum speciosum*—also known as Tiger orchid—is the largest orchid in the world. Weighing up to 2,000 lbs, it can produce up to 10,000 flowers on a mature plant.

Oreos®

🦢 More than 7.5 billion Oreos® are consumed every year. If all the Oreos® ever made were stacked, they'd reach the moon and back more than five times.

🦢 The Oreo® is the #1 selling cookie in China and after research proved that wafers were the fastest growing snack, Kraft redesigned the cookie to look like a wafer while retaining the same taste of the original cookie.

🦢 Brazil has a very similar cookie to Oreo® called "Negresco," produced by Nestlé.

🦢 In 1998, the Oreo® packaging featured the OUD symbol which means the cookie was made kosher.

🦢 Along with deep-fried Twinkies and chocolate bars, deep-fried Oreos® are novel treats at carnivals and fairs. The cookies are dipped in batter and deep-fried for thirty seconds.

🦢 Introduced in Canada and sold for a limited time in the United States, the Strawberry Milkshake Oreo boasted an Oreo® cookie with strawberry flavoring.

O

Ostrich

- A female ostrich can determine her own eggs amongst others in a communal nest.

- Ostriches are so powerful that a single kick at a predator, such as a lion, could be fatal.

- At a speed of 40 miles per hour, an ostrich can outrun most predators such as such as leopards, lions, and hyenas.

- Ostrich meat is a red meat that resembles beef and can be cooked in the same way. Unlike beef though, ostrich is very low in cholesterol, calories, and fat.

- There are approximately two million ostriches walking the face of the Earth and they can be successfully farmed from the coldest climates of Alaska to the warmest in central Africa.

Oxygen

❧ The average brain makes up 2% of a person's total body weight, but it requires 25% of all oxygen used by the body.

❧ Most of us know that H_2O is a compound made of hydrogen and oxygen, but few realize that oxygen dissolves into water, which is the oxygen that fish and other marine creatures breathe.

❧ Oxygen attaches to red blood cells, which creates the bright red color of our blood. Once red blood cells release the oxygen and pick up carbon dioxide, human blood turns a dark red or maroon color.

❧ Heavy breathing…Humans inhale more than 6 billion tons of oxygen annually.

❧ A mature leafy tree can produce as much oxygen in one season as ten people inhale in one year.

O

Pac-Man

- While having dinner, a programmer named Toru Iwatani was searching for inspiration for a game character. He saw a pizza pie with a slice missing and the Pac-man was born.

- The game was originally called Puckman, derived from the Japanese phrase *pakupaku*, which describes the motion of eating or munching. When Bally/Midway brought the game to America, they had it changed to Pac-man.

- *Pac-man* is the best selling video game in history.

- Pac-Man travels 20% faster in areas where the dots have been eaten.

- Atari passed up the rights to the game, claiming it was too simple.

- The first *Pac-Man* World Championship was held in New York City on June 5, 2007. Ten competitors from eight countries vied for the champion title, which eventually went to Carlos Daniel Borrego of Mexico. His prize was an Xbox 360 console, specially decorated with Pac-Man artwork and signed by Toru Iwatani.

Parthenon

❧ The Parthenon has no straight lines and contains no mortar.

❧ The Parthenon is a temple located on the Acropolis, a hill overlooking the city of Athens, Greece. Its name literally means "virgin's place" and was a temple for the Goddess Athena.

❧ Approximately 13,400 stones were used to build the Parthenon.

❧ The frieze of the Parthenon is one of the first to depict common people along with the Gods, reflecting the Greek love and belief in democratic principles.

❧ Nashville, TN, is home to a full-scale replica of the original Parthenon. It was built in 1897 as part of the Tennessee Centennial Exposition.

P

Parton, Dolly

🐦 "I'm not offended by dumb blonde jokes because I know that I'm not dumb. I also know I'm not blonde."—Dolly Parton

🐦 "9 to 5" is the theme song to the 1980 film starring Parton along with Jane Fonda and Lily Tomlin. The song reached #1 on the country charts as well as on the pop and adult contemporary ones, making Parton one of the few female country singers to have a #1 across three charts simultaneously.

🐦 Parton has performed on a top-40 country hit in each of the last five decades.

🐦 Parton can play the autoharp, banjo, drums, dulcimer, guitar, harmonica, fiddle, and piano.

🐦 At the tender age of four, Parton was already composing songs and her mother would often write down the music when she heard Dolly singing in the house.

🐦 Opened in 1986 and co-owned by the country music legend, *Dollywood* in Tennessee brings in approximately 2.5 million visitors annually.

🐦 Dolly Parton's 40DD breasts are nothing short of inspiring. In 1996, a sheep was the first mammal to be cloned. Since the sheep was cloned from a cell taken from the mammary gland of an adult ewe, stockmen came up with the idea to name the lamb after the famed country singer.

P

Pasta

❧ The names of various forms of pasta all have meanings—whether descriptive, humorous, or even pedantic. For example, the term spaghetti is derived from the Italian word *spago*, or "string."

❧ *Pasta in brodo* is simply translated as "pasta in broth" while the term *pasta asciutta* translates literally to the "dry" pasta, the kind of pasta which is not designed for broth—spaghetti, vermicelli, rigatoni, lasagne, etc.

❧ Records indicate that the Chinese were eating pasta as early as 5,000 BC.

❧ On September 13, 2007, Italian consumer groups called a one-day strike against buying pasta in protest of the increasing costs that had seen its price rise by almost 20%.

❧ When Thomas Jefferson was the U.S. Ambassador to France, he once dined in Naples, Italy, and fell in love with a certain dish. He immediately ordered crates of "macaroni" as well as a pasta-making machine and shipped them to the States. This is why some say that Jefferson introduced macaroni to the States.

❧ The average person in Italy consumes more than 51 pounds of pasta every year as opposed to the average North American who eats about 15.5 in that same time.

P

Pentagon

🌿 As one of the world's largest buildings, the Pentagon is twice the size of the Merchandise Mart in Chicago, and has three times the floor space of the Empire State Building in New York.

🌿 23,000 military and civilian employees contributed to the planning and execution of the defense of the U.S.

🌿 Dial in...More than 200,000 telephone calls are made every day through phone lines that are connected by 100,000 miles of telephone cable at the Pentagon.

🌿 There are 17.5 miles of corridors, but it only takes seven minutes to walk between any two points in the building.

P

Pepper

🐦 *Achoo!* Whether it's white, black, or green, pepper contains an alkaloid of pyridine called "piperine," which acts as an irritant if it gets into the nose. It irritates the nerve endings inside the mucous membrane, and causes you to sneeze.

🐦 The pungency and fiery hotness associated with chili peppers come from the compound capsaicin in the internal partitions of the fruit.

🐦 Looking rather green…all sweet bell peppers start out green, and change color as they ripen. Thus, red, orange, and yellow peppers are more expensive because they require more time to ripen and also have a shorter storage life.

🐦 In 2009, the cops at a North Carolina college used pepper spray to tame a rowdy crowd after a mass snowball fight got out of control. Police stated they were forced to use the pepper spray because unruly students were rushing the officers. One student was arrested for throwing a snowball at a cop who had his back turned to him.

🐦 It may seem like an unlikely pair, but strawberries and black pepper complement each other. A hint of black pepper accentuates the berries by adding a subtle warmth and heat…when used sparingly of course.

P

Perfume

  ❧ The word originates from the Latin word *per fumum*, which means "through smoke."

  ❧ In 2007, Italian archaeologists claimed to have sniffed out the world's oldest perfumes on the island reputed to be the birthplace of Aphrodite. Remnants of the perfumes were extracted from an ancient factory that was part of a larger complex at Pyrgos.

  ❧ Common ingredients added to perfumes include ginger, grapefruit, musk, peppercorns, mandarin peel, fig leaves, rose, watercress, bamboo, clementine, vanilla, honeysuckle, and green tea.

  ❧ To preserve perfumes, it is best to keep them in light, tight aluminium bottles and to refrigerate them at low temperatures between 3–7°C.

  ❧ Perfume fragrances last longer on people with oily skin because their skin has more natural moisture content to hold the fragrance.

  ❧ Chanel No. 5 has been around since 1921 and is the company's most popular perfume. They estimate that one bottle is sold worldwide every 55 seconds.

  ❧ What's that smell? At www.perpetualkid.com, a crayon-scented perfume will have you re-living your preschool days of a bygone childhood. If you want a slightly more sophisticated scent, consider the other perfumes in the collection, which include vinyl, vanilla cake batter, and sushi.

Picasso, Pablo

❧ One of the most celebrated artists in the world, Pablo Picasso was so poor early in his career that he stayed warm by burning some of his drawings.

❧ Picasso was named after just a few saints and relatives. He was baptized Pablo Diego José Francisco de Paula Juan Nepomuceno María de los Remedios Cipriano de la Santísima Trinidad Martyr Patricio Clito Ruíz y Picasso.

❧ His first word was "piz," short for *lapiz*, the Spanish word for pencil.

❧ Picasso completed his first painting—*Le picador*—when he was only nine years old. He was 13 years old when he had his first exhibit, showing his paintings in the back room of an umbrella store.

❧ Though he may have been a brilliant artist, he was an awful student who rebelled against authority and spent much of his time in detention. "For being a bad student I was banished to the 'calaboose,' a bare cell with whitewashed walls and a bench to sit on. I liked it there, because I took along a sketch pad and drew incessantly..."

❧ In 2006, casino mogul Steve Wynn was prepared to sell the painting "Le Rêve," for $139 million. The day before the sale was to be completed, he accidentally put his elbow through the canvas. Suffice to say, he kept the painting.

P

Pigeons

In Europe between the 16th and 18th century, pigeon poo was prized as an invaluable resource. As fertilizer, it was considered to be more potent than farmyard manure and armed guards were stationed in front of dovecotes (pigeon houses) to stop thieves from stealing it.

In the early 19th century, the Rothschild family set up a network of homing pigeons to carry information between its financial houses throughout Europe. This method of delivery provided to be quicker and more efficient than any other carrier at the time. The family became one of richest and most famous of the time, due in part to the ability to send and receive information ahead of the competitors.

As a pigeon has monocular vision, it bobs its head for depth of perception. The pigeon's eyes generally work better with stationary images.

Male and female parent pigeons can produce a unique substance known as "pigeon milk" to feed their hatchlings during the first week of life.

While most birds sip water and then throw back their heads so it trickles down their throats, pigeons use their beaks like straws to suck up the water.

Pony Express

❧ The Pony Express was an expedited mail service crossing the North American continent from April 1860 to October 1861, using horseback riders to courier deliveries. Mail traveled from the Atlantic to the Pacific coast in about ten days.

❧ Each rider traveled about 75 miles and then handed the mail to the next rider.

❧ 183 men were known to have ridden for the Pony Express during its 18 months of operation. The youngest Pony Express rider was Charlie Miller, aka Broncho Charlie, who was just 11 years old.

❧ Riders were paid $100 per month.

❧ One job ad in California read: "Wanted. Young, skinny, wiry fellows. Not over 18. Must be expert riders. Willing to risk death daily. Orphans preferred."

P

Post-it® Notes

- Artist Melynda Schwier-Gierard used 60,000 1½ in × 2 in Post-it® Notes to create an art piece of uniquely textured, wall-sized panels.

- In 1998, a workplace study showed that the average professional receives eleven Post-it® messages a day.

- Approximately 506,880,000 Post-it® Notes would be required to encircle the world once (based on the earth's circumference of 24,000 miles and using 2-⅞ in square Post-it® Notes).

- Esquire magazine named Post-it® Note inventor Art Fry one of "The 100 Best People in the World."

- The name "Post-it" and the signature canary yellow color are trademarks of company 3M.

P

Pregnancy

❧ The number of caesarean deliveries has increased by more than 40% in the last decade to 27% of births, the highest rate ever reported in the United States.

❧ Tuesday is the most popular day for babies to be born and Saturday the least. This could be due to the fact that many doctors do not schedule C-sections for Saturdays.

❧ In 1945, a Mrs. Hunter had been pregnant 375 days (instead of the normal 280) before her baby was born at Los Angeles' Methodist Hospital. Her daughter, Penny Diana, weighed only 6 lb and 15 oz.

❧ According to ancient Chinese beliefs, Pregnancy is considered a "hot" condition, so to balance the scale between "ying and yang" cold foods must be consumed throughout pregnancy. On the contrary, post partum is considered a "cold" condition due to blood loss during labor, so the mother should consume hot foods only.

P

❧ Pregnant women should avoid eating more than 12 ounces of fish each week. Fish—including swordfish, shark, king mackerel, and tilefish—may contain high amounts of mercury, a metal that can be toxic to babies, children, and even adults.

Prohibition

➤ An estimated 75% of the liquor that was smuggled into the U.S. during prohibition arrived along a route from the mouth of the Lake Erie and St. Claire Rivers. This was eventually nicknamed the "Windsor-Detroit Funnel."

➤ When prohibition was repealed, beer was the first legal alcoholic drink made available on April 7, 1933. Other alcoholic beverages were made legal December 5, 1933.

➤ In 1904, North Dakota was a prohibition state but Montana wasn't. In Sidney, MO, a bar was built on the state line so one could buy a drink in Montana and drink it in North Dakota.

➤ Pilsner Urquell was the number one import beer in the U.S. before Prohibition.

➤ Al Capone, also known as Scarface, was the most famous figure during the Prohibition Era for his control of large portions of the Chicago underworld. Capone was making $10 million per year in revenue through the sales of bootleg alcohol, racketeering, gambling, and prostitution…tax-free, of course.

➤ Templeton Rye Whiskey was said to be Al Capone's whiskey of choice.

P

Q-tips®

🍃 Leo Gerstenzang invented the cotton swab in the 1920s after attaching wads of cotton to toothpicks. His product was originally named "Baby Gays."

🍃 The word "Q-tip" is an abbreviation for "Quality tip," though the Q once stood for "Quilted."

🍃 Nearly 3 out of 4 Americans stick cotton swabs in their ears despite the package's instructions against it.

🍃 Q-tips® cotton swabs are the most popular product for babies in the United States.

🍃 The website www.instructables.com provides instructions for making a Q-tip gun, which can launch Q-tips® anywhere between 30–50 ft.

Q

Quail

- Dirty bird! The California Quail is known to live in convoys and to enjoy the occasional community dust bath.

- It's true love or nothing for the Mountain Quail and Gambel's Quail—they are both monogamous.

- Also called the Blue Quail or Cottontop, a Scaled Quail has a feather pattern similar to scales.

- The sex of a quail can be determined by the feather shape and coloration on the head and wings. The males have black and white stripes along the side of their heads while the stripes on a female's head are brown and sandy.

- The California Quail digests vegetation with the help of protozoan in its intestine. Chicks acquire the protozoa by pecking at the feces of adults.

- Quail eggs are a delicacy in many countries around the world. In Colombia, a single hard-boiled quail egg is a popular topping for hot dogs and hamburgers.

Q

Quakers

❧ "Quakers" earned their name from the trembling which occurred when the Spirit moved them.

❧ Quakerism is a way of life rather than a set of beliefs. They seek divine experience directly, within themselves, and through their relationships with those around them. These encounters provide Quakers a meaning and purpose.

❧ Quakers are not Amish, Anabaptists, Shakers, or Puritans…they also no longer dress like the man on the Quaker Oats box.

❧ The UK alone has approximately 25,000 Quakers.

❧ Charity organizations such as Amnesty International, Oxfam and Relate all started as fledgling enterprises founded by Quakers.

❧ Famous Quakers included British surgeon Joseph Lister, father of antiseptic surgery; Lucretia Mott, women's rights/anti-slavery activist, and former President Richard Nixon.

Q

Queen Elizabeth II

🍃 Since 1917, the Sovereign has sent congratulatory messages to people celebrating their 100th and 105th birthday and every birthday thereafter. The message consists of a card with a personalized greeting and a facsimile signature. The Queen has sent 100,000 telegrams to centenarians in the UK and the Commonwealth.

🍃 The Queen has a meeting with the Prime Minister of England every Tuesday.

🍃 Hot doggity! The Queen received a corgi for her 18th birthday and has owned more than 30 ever since. Her Majesty currently has five corgis: Monty, Willow, Holly, Emma, and Linnet.

🍃 The Crown owns all mute swans in the kingdom because of an outdated quirk from the 12th century. Though the Queen only exercises her rights on specific stretches of the River Thames and its surrounding tributaries, the Crown can take action to prosecute those guilty of harming a swan. In 2006, Shamsu Miah was so hungry during Ramadan that he killed a swan and was confined to jail for two months.

🍃 The Queen has received a number of unusual gifts during her reign, many of which include live animals. The more exotic animals such as the jaguar and a sloth from Brazil have been placed in the care of the London zoo, but she has also received two black beavers from Canada. Other odd gifts include pineapples, eggs, a box of snail shells, a grove of maple trees, and 7 kg of prawns.

Quiff

❧ The quiff is a hairstyle that combines the 1950s pompadour hairstyle, the flattop, and occasionally, a mohawk.

❧ The hairstyle was trendy during the British "Teddy Boy" movement, but became popular again in Europe with early psychobilly acts including The Meteors, Demented Are Go, and other groups of the early 80s.

❧ The Japanese Punch perm, a favorite among Yakuza members, bears a strong similarity to this hairstyle.

❧ Famous quiffs include those of Morrissey, Tintin, Elvis Presley, Conan O'Brian and the former Brazilian president, Itamar Franco.

❧ A quiff can also be used to describe a promiscuous woman.

❧ To attain the perfect quiff, one should first wash and towel dry the hair. Then, while the hair is still slightly damp, apply medium-hold gel to the roots. Use a blow dryer to heat the roots so the hair is lifted off the face. Finally, lift the quiff high at the front.

Q

Rabbits

- Rabbits are nocturnal creatures that are most active between dusk and dawn.

- When a rabbit is happy, it will click its teeth. If it is angry toward a human or another rabbit, it will grunt.

- Rabbits are not rodents. They belong to a family called "lagomorphs."

- The mating ritual among the European rabbits is almost without motion and can last more than thirty minutes. Males will fight each other by squirting urine and even using their teeth to castrate one another in pursuit of their female companions. Occasionally, a male will have his genitalia gnawed.

- According to Chinese astrology, people born in the Year of the Rabbit are articulate, talented, and ambitious. They are also considered patient, kind, and virtuous, and even better than that—financially lucky. They are most compatible with those born in the years of the Sheep, Pig, and Dog.

- An American rabbit named "Nipper's Geromino" has the longest ears on record, measuring 31.125."

Rain

🐦 A drizzle occurs when drops of rain are less than half a millimeter.

🐦 There are three general types of rain: orographic, frontal, and convective. Also known as showers, convective rain generally lasts for less than one hour.

🐦 The world record for rainfall was 1825 mm (over 6 ft!) at Foc-Foc, Reunion in the Indian Ocean.

🐦 Mawsynram in the state of Meghalaya, India, is known as the wettest city in the world. The average annual rainfall is 12,000 mm (39.37 ft).

🐦 Feel the need for speed? A raindrop falls at 600 ft per minute or 7 mph.

🐦 A raindrop is actually circular but appears oval because gravitation pulls on the front as the raindrop is falling.

🐦 Forks, Washington is the rainiest city in the continental United States…but it really made it on the map after becoming the home of the vampires in Stephenie Meyer's bestselling *Twilight* series.

R

Rainforest

❧ Every second, an area of the rainforest comparable to a size of a football field is being destroyed.

❧ A tropical rainforest can be so densely packed with trees that rain falling on the canopy can take as long as 10 minutes to touch the ground.

❧ In moist South American rain forests, sloths move slowly enough for algae to grow in their fur.

❧ Tropical rainforests circle the Earth's equator like a belt, maintaining an average constant temperature of 80°F and acquiring 160–400 in of rain each year.

❧ Nearly half of world's original four billion acres of rainforest have now disappeared. The amount lost is equivalent to the combined size of Washington, Idaho, California, Nevada, and Arizona.

R

Rambo

❧ The movie was an adaptation of the novel written by award-winning Canadian author, David Morrell. In the book, the character of Rambo kills many of his pursuers, while in the film he is not directly responsible for any of the deaths. Before filming, Sylvester Stallone felt the character of John Rambo needed to be more sympathetic.

❧ *Rambo: First Blood II* was the first film where Rambo killed while shirtless. Total number of casualties? 46.

❧ In Japanese, the word "rambo" means "violence."

❧ Before Stallone was signed onto the project, the film studio Warner Bros had considered Clint Eastwood, Steve McQueen, Al Pacino, and Dustin Hoffman for the role.

❧ With its $63 million-dollar budget, *Rambo III* was the most expensive film ever made at the time of its release.

R

Rats

◈ The Karni Mata temple in the town of Deshnoke, India, is known to be a temple of rats. Goddess Karni is thought to be a reincarnation of Goddess Durga. The rats in this temple are worshipped as they are considered to be the spirits of Goddess Karni's followers. The priests who maintain this ancient temple provide the rats with food.

◈ Rats can live without water for an even longer duration than camels.

◈ An experiment was done in which a marked rat was left on one of the islands of New Zealand. Within a few days, the same rat was found on another island 400 meters away from the original one. They can swim in the water for as long as 36 hours.

◈ Hold the cheddar! Contrary to popular belief, rats do not like cheese; in fact, they are lactose intolerant.

◈ Rats will eat their own feces, strictly for the nutritional value.

◈ Rats may not have gallbladders or tonsils, but all are born with belly buttons.

◈ During its receptivity period, the female rat can mate around 500 times and with 500 different partners! Each period lasts around 6 hours and occurs 15 times in one year. In fact, a pair of mating rats could produce 1,500 more rats in only one year if all of their offspring survive.

Rice

❧ The Chinese word for rice is the same word used for food.

❧ There are more than 40,000 different varieties of rice. Of those varieties, more than 100 grow worldwide (with the exception of Antarctica) but only 10% of them are marketed and sold.

❧ Rice is traditionally thrown at the bride and groom at weddings as it symbolizes life and fertility. These days, confetti is often used instead of rice.

❧ Grains of rice added to a salt container keep the salt flowing freely.

❧ The "wild rice" marketed and sold in supermarkets across North America is a type of grass called *zinzania aquatica*. It has no relation to the rice plant at all.

❧ 5,000 liters of water is required to produce 1 kg of rice.

R

Rio de Janeiro

- Rio De Janeiro is home to the largest and second largest urban forests in the world: *Floresta da Tijuca* (or "Tijuca Forest") and the forest in *Parque Estadual da Pedra Branca* (or "White Stone State Park").

- Many of Brazil's most notorious *favelas*, or shantytowns, are located in Rio de Janeiro. They are ridden by sewage, crime, and hygiene problems. In Rio, one in every four *cariocas* (as Rio's inhabitants are called) lives in a *favela*, which is not recognized in the city as a legal entity.

- Rio has 50 km (31 miles) of beaches spread out along the coast of the state.

- Carnival festivities in Rio de Janeiro date back as early as 1723 in the form of *Entrudo*. The basic idea was to get everyone soaking wet: people would go onto the streets with buckets of water and lime, prepared to make any passerby a potential victim. It was so popular that even the emperors took part in the charades. There is a documented record, however, of a woman being arrested in 1855 for throwing a lime at Dom Pedro I's escorts. Authorities frowned upon the lack of control, and eventually *Entrudo* was outlawed.

- Duran Duran's hit single "Rio" was inspired by the band's tour to Brazil. The music video was shot over the course of three days in May 1982 on the island of Antigua, and encapsulates the glamour and excess associated with the decade.

Roller Coasters

✦ As a practical application, NASA announced that it would build a roller coaster to help astronauts escape the Aries I launch pad in case of an emergency.

✦ In Japan, roller coasters are very popular at amusements parks and are known as jet coasters.

✦ The "4th Dimension" is a term used to describe a style of roller coaster where riders are positioned on either side of the track, in seats capable of spinning on a horizontal axis. An example of this is the "X Roller Coaster" at Six Flags Magic Mountain.

✦ Six Flags Great Adventures boasts the fastest roller coaster in the world. Kingda Ka, the "rocket coaster", accelerates to 128 mph in 3.5 seconds and towers at 456 ft, making it the tallest, fastest roller coaster in the world.

✦ A man who did not talk for six years because of shell shock spoke his first words after a ride on the Coney Island Cyclone. He told his friend, "I feel sick."

✦ In addition to wallets, change, and keys, some of the more unusual items found under roller coaster tracks are glass eyes, fake legs, brassieres, and false teeth.

R

The Rolling Stones

 Growing up in the outskirts of London, Mick Jagger was a choirboy who was a huge fan of musicians like Muddy Waters, Leadbelly, and Chuck Berry while the young Keith Richards was a fan of classic blues, jazz, and R&B. They attended the same elementary school together but didn't meet up until their later teens, when Mick was a student at the prestigious London School of Economics.

 "Sympathy for the Devil" is not a song about devil worshipping. It was inspired by Mikhail Bulgakov's classic novel, *The Master and Margarita*, and also included references to WWII and the Kennedy assassinations.

 In February 1977, Royal Canadian Mounted Police arrested Keith and Anita Pallenberg for possession of heroin, cocaine, and hashish. Keith was sentenced to community service, which included a benefit show for the Canadian National Institute for the Blind. He was once quoted to say, "I never had a problem with drugs, only with cops."

 "Gimme Shelter" is the first song on the "Let it Bleed" album, and also the title of the Rolling Stones 1969 tour film. This documentary is renowned for capturing most of the violence of the Stones tour-ending free concert at Altamont Speedway in California. A disruption between members of the Hell's Angels biker gang and the audience culminated in the murder of a young fan named Meredith Hunter.

 The song "You Don't Move Me" was written by Keith Richards as an angry response to Mick Jagger's decision to go solo.

The Roman Empire

ℜ The Roman Apicius published the first documented recipe book in 62 AD. Titled *De Re Coquinaria*, it described the feasts enjoyed by the Emperor Claudius.

ℜ At the height of the Roman Empire in the second century, the land area was roughly the size of the U.S. today. The population was estimated somewhere between 70–100 million people.

ℜ Poisonous lead was used as a sweetening agent by the Romans. The sweetener, sapa, was made by reducing sour wine in lead pans. The lead from the pans combined with the wine to create lead acetate which remained in the final sweetening product.

ℜ The city of London, the capital of the United Kingdom, was founded by the Romans under the name Londinium.

ℜ Emperor Justinian bribed two Persian monks who were living in China to smuggle silkworm eggs to him in hallow bamboo canes. Thus, Constantinople began silk production around 550 AD. All the silk-producing caterpillars in Europe are descendants of these worms.

R

Rubik's Cube®

<ul>
<li>A Hungarian by the name of Erno Rubik invented the Cube in the spring of 1974. He created it as a working model to help explain three-dimensional geometry, and this led to the creation of the world's best-selling toy.</li>

<li>It's hip to be square...at the peak of the Rubik's cube craze, an estimated one-fifth of the world's population had played the Cube.</li>

<li>Rubikcubism is an avant-garde artistic movement in which Rubik's cubes are used as a medium to create art.</li>

<li>In May 2007, Thibaut Jacquinot of France became the first person to complete the Cube in less than 10 seconds in open competition. Erik Akkersdijk set the current world record for a single solve at the 2008 Czech Open with a time of 7.08 seconds.</li>

<li>In 1981, a seven-year-old Norwegian boy named Lars-Erik Anderson was one of the youngest Cube solvers.</li>

<li>Initially, Rubik considered variations of a 2 × 2 in cube, but concluded that the simplest and most workable model was the 3 × 3 × 3 in cube.</li>
</ul>

R

Rugby

◆ Rugby balls have always been oval. The boys at Rugby School use inflated pigs bladders for the balls, which are, by nature, oval in shape.

◆ Until 1877, international rugby teams had 20 players on each side, as opposed to 15.

◆ The very first match at Twickenham Stadium took place in 1909, a stadium that can hold 74,000 spectators.

◆ The School House team of 1839 was the first team to adopt a uniform. All the players wore red velvet caps during matches, which were attended by the Dowager, Queen Adelaide. The cap was eventually adopted by rugby clubs, then by England and then other Unions as a symbolic embodiment of national and international achievement.

R

◆ A match between Whitby and Corby was forced to end prematurely in 1989 because the Corby players were too drunk to continue. The referee called a halt to proceedings seven minutes into the second half with Corby already trailing 80–0.

Saffron

❧ Saffron, the most expensive spice in the world, is the stamen of the saffron crocus flower. Each saffron crocus flower has 3 stigmas and about 80,000 flowers (240,000). The stigmas are needed to make one pound of saffron. By the time saffron gets to retail stores, it retails for $600 to $2000 per pound.

❧ The ancient Assyrians used saffron for medicinal purposes while the Greeks and Romans used it to scent baths. The saturated burnt orange color made it a common dye as well.

❧ In 1444, any merchant caught selling adulterated saffron in Bavaria was burned alive.

S

❧ Cheap "saffron" is often a hack version made from safflower, turmeric, or marigold.

❧ Stay clear of the Meadow saffron, a poisonous plant unrelated to saffron.

Sahara Desert

❧ The Sahara is the second largest desert in the world (Antarctica is the first) and occupies approximately 10% of Africa. The total area is more than 3,500,000 square miles. Temperatures can reach up to 122°F (50°C).

❧ In the summer of 2008, archaeologists discovered the remains of a tiny woman and two children who were laid to rest on a bed of flowers 5,000 years ago in the Sahara. Their skeletons were found in a cemetery and provided clues to two civilizations that lived there when the region was moist, green, and fertile.

❧ Hot, hot, heat! The *Marathon des Sables*, also known as Marathon of the Sands, is a six-day, 151-mile endurance race across the Sahara Desert in Morocco. In 2007, the race claimed the life of a 49-year-old French runner, Bernard Juke, who was discovered in his tent. He died of a heart attack.

❧ Nomads make up the majority of people living in the Sahara Desert. The first nomads came to the region after domestic animals were introduced in the Sahara 7,000 years ago. Researchers believe that sheep and goats were brought by the Caspian culture of northern Africa.

❧ The last thing on one's mind would be working up a sweat in the desert…or so we thought. Dune boarding is a novel activity growing in popularity among sports adventure enthusiasts. It adheres to the principles of snowboarding but instead of snow, one carves on sand.

S

Saints

 St. Simeon was called *Stylites*, meaning "pillar-dweller." He was a fifth-century Syrian saint who spent the last thirty years of his life sitting on top of a pillar 70 ft high.

 They're always after me lucky charms! St. Patrick was not actually Irish but British—most likely from modern-day Wales. He was only in Ireland after being kidnapped by Irish raiders. Upon escaping and becoming a priest and a bishop, Patrick eventually returned to Ireland as a missionary. He was made the patron saint of Ireland because of his success in converting the Irish.

 The seven deadly sins—anger, covetousness, envy, gluttony, lust, pride, and sloth—are not enumerated in the Bible; they were first set forth by St. Thomas Aquinas.

 St. Adrian Nicomedia is the patron saint of arms dealers. He is commonly represented armed, with an anvil in his hands or at his feet.

 St. Anthony the Abbot is the patron saint of both pig herders and skin diseases. He is often depicted with a pig because pork fat was used as a treatment for skin ailments.

Saliva

❧ A mouth can produce 1 liter of saliva a day.

❧ There is no flavor to food without saliva. In order for a person to taste food, chemicals from the food must first dissolve in saliva, which can then be detected by receptors on taste buds.

❧ Human saliva is 99.5% water while the remaining composition is comprised of electrolytes, mucus, antibacterial compounds, and various enzymes.

❧ The dander zone...the cat allergy is caused by the protein in the cat's saliva. When a cat grooms itself, it deposits this protein onto its fur, and the protein then may be transferred to upholstery and carpets.

❧ Rabies is transmitted when the virus is present in the saliva of an infected animal and penetrates the skin through a bite.

S

Salmon

- A female spring Chinook salmon can carry more than 4,000 eggs.

- The oldest salmon fossil found is 50 million years old.

- Salmon do not eat any food during the time they swim upstream to spawn.

- The longest known trip ever taken by a salmon was a Chinook salmon that traveled 3,845 km (2,389 miles) upstream to spawn.

- When salmon are swimming upstream, they can jump two yards into the air.

S

Salt

❧ Salt is composed of two poisons: sodium and chlorine.

❧ Adding a little salt to a grapefruit reduces the acidity and makes the grapefruit taste sweeter.

❧ The City of Salt is an underground city in Wieliczka, Poland, carved completely out of solid salt. Beneath Wieliczka is one of the world's largest salt mines, which, until recently, had been producing salt since medieval times. The mines span seven levels, the deepest of which is 1,000 ft below the surface. They also contain about 75 miles of passageways and chambers, plus 16 lakes.

❧ In the U.S., only 6% of the salt used is for food; another 17% is used for de-icing streets and highways in the winter months.

❧ In the early 19th century, salt was four times more expensive than beef on the frontier.

❧ Salt lowers the temperature at which water freezes and melts. Pure water freezes and melts at 0°C. However, adding salt to water will lower its freezing point. A water with extreme salinity (such as the very salty lake waters at Death Valley, CA) may freeze and melt at temperatures as low as −20 to −30°C. This is why it is added to icy roads in order to melt the ice.

❧ During the Roman Empire, Roman soldiers were issued salt, or, alternatively, a sum of money to buy salt, a *salarium*, from which the word "salary" is derived.

S

San Francisco

❧ When the first mayor announced San Francisco as the new name of his town, only 469 residents lived there including Ohlone Indians, Americans, Spanish Californians, Hawaiians, Europeans, South Americans, and New Zealanders.

❧ Some landmark films shot in San Francisco include *The Maltese Falcon*, *Vertigo*, *The Birds*, and *The Graduate*.

❧ Blue note…denim jeans were invented in San Francisco for the Gold Rush. Miners were in need of durable, comfortable clothing.

❧ "I Left My Heart In San Francisco" was written in 1954 by the gay couple, Douglass Cross and George Cory, though it was Tony Bennett's version in 1962 which made the song famous.

❧ Fortune cookies were invented in San Fran! The Japanese Hagiwara family invented "Chinese" fortune cookies at Chinatown's Ross Alley fortune cookie factory to be served at Golden Gate Park's Tea Garden.

❧ *Alcatraz* is the Spanish word for "pelican."

S

Santa Claus

🦋 The original Saint Nicholas of Myria was the patron saint of thieves.

🦋 Santa Claus's workshop was first depicted by the cartoonist Thomas Nast in 1866.

🦋 Santa Claus goes by several aliases depending on where he is in the world. In China, he's known as "Shengdan Laoren;" in the UK, "Father Christmas;" in France as "Pere Noel;" and in some Latin countries, he is called "El Niesus" or "Papa Noel." During the Communist years of Russia, he was hailed as "Father Frost."

🦋 In some countries, including Germany, it is said that the Baby Jesus is the bearer of gifts, not Santa.

🦋 The Canadian Postal System has an official address for Santa Claus where children can write to Santa and receive a response, no matter what language you speak or what country you are from. This address is: Santa Claus, North Pole, Canada HOH OHO.

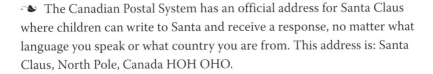

S

Seafood

- The giant clam of the South Seas, also known as *tridacna gigas,* can make one hundred gallons of chowder. It can reach giant lengths of over 4 ft and weigh in excess of 500 lbs.

- The Japanese spider crab, *Macrocheira kaempferi,* is the largest known arthropod. Fully grown, it can boast a 13 ft leg span, a body size of up to 15 in, and a weight of up to 44 lbs. It is believed to have a life expectancy of up to 100 years and tastes incredible with butter.

- Lobsters actually come in an array of colors—blue, light yellow, greenish-brown, gray, dusty orange, calico, and some even have spots. Despite its original coloring, a lobster always turns red when cooked.

- An average oyster filters over 50 gallons of water each day by sucking it in and spitting it back out again. This action allows the oyster to gather food particles from the water while filtering out things like gold, mercury, arsenic, and lead.

- The scallop is a hermaphrodite. The shell contains both the female and the male gonad, but it is quite normal for the hermaphrodite scallop to fertilize with other scallops.

Sex

❧ Beauty marks were originally used to cover scars left by a 17th century smallpox epidemic. As the epidemic subsided, women continued to use beauty marks to acknowledge courtiers. A mark near the mouth beckoned a willingness to flirt whereas one on the right cheek signified she was already married. One on the left cheek indicated engagement and one near the corner of the eye gave the green light to a red-hot night.

❧ On a high note…around 2,300 BC, the ancient Sumerians used one of the earliest forms of contraceptives. Balls of opium were inserted into the vagina and not only would it protect them from impregnation, but it got them high as well.

❧ In Greek mythology, Priapus was the god of fertility and male genitilia. He was best known for his huge, permanently erect penis, which gave rise to the medical term "priapism," a painful condition where the erect penis does not return to its normal state within four hours.

S

❧ The 1933 film *Ecstasy*, starring Hedy Lamarr, was the first film to show a woman/couple having an orgasm during sex.

❧ 52% of Icelanders own a vibrator.

❧ In Japan, the age of consent is 13.

❧ In a recent US study, 29% of American men report having 15 or more female sexual partners in a lifetime. Only 9% percent of women report having sex with 15 or more men.

The Sex Pistols

- The group only released just one studio album in the short span of their career. The remaining seven were a combination of live albums, compilations, and a movie soundtrack.

- The group was so controversial that band members and fans became victims of physical attacks.

- The band was first known as "The Strand," then "The Swankers" before it evolved to The Sex Pistols.

- In the film *Sid and Nancy*, Gary Oldman lost so much weight to play Sid Vicious that he ended up hospitalized.

S

- John Lydon—more commonly known as Johnny Rotten—appeared as a defendant on *Judge Judy* in 1997. A former tour/session drummer Robert Williams filed a suit against Lydon for $5,000 in unpaid fees and civil battery. The case was dismissed.

- The remaining members of the punk band refused to attend their own induction into the Rock and Roll Hall of Fame, claiming in a handwritten note that the institution was "urine in wine."

Silk

❧ 5,500 silkworms are needed to produce 2.2 lbs (1 kg) of raw silk.

❧ Silk are the fibers that silkworms produce to make their cocoons. Silkworms are not actually worms but silk-producing larvae or caterpillars that belong to several species of moths.

❧ The silk-making process was invented by the Chinese thousands of years ago. They produce approximately half of the silk made in the entire world.

❧ The fluffy white cocoon spun by a silkworm is one long continuous silk filament that when unwound can span as long as 1,600 yards.

❧ The finest silk comes from the silkworms produced by the Bombyx mori moth, which cannot fly or see. One moth will lay approximately 500 eggs over a 4–6 day period and dies shortly thereafter. These eggs are very tiny, about as big as the point of a pin.

❧ It takes silk from more than 2,000 cocoons to produce a single kimono.

S

Singapore

🐦 The U.S. is 15,000 times larger than Singapore, which is one of the 20 smallest countries in the world. The total land area of the country is only 682.7 square kilometers.

🐦 Is it a small world after all? Next to Monaco, Singapore is the most densely populated country in the world. There are 6,430 people per square kilometer.

🐦 "Singlish" is a regional Singaporean language, which combines English with the odd phrase of Chinese, Malay, and even Tamil.

🐦 Singaporeans give birth more in October than any other month of the year.

🐦 Jurong Bird Park is the world's highest man-made waterfall, standing at 30 meters.

S

Skin

- A square inch of skin on the human hand has 72 feet of nerves.

- An average person's skin weighs twice as much as his brain.

- A person has shed 40 lbs of skin by the age of 70.

- The skin can release as much as three gallons of sweat a day in hot weather.

- 70% of the dust in a home consists of shed human skin.

S

Sky

❧ In 1867, scientist John Tyndall first discovered why the sky is blue. When a flashlight is shone through clean filtered air, the beam cannot be seen. With normal air, it can. He concluded that one sees the light beams because the air is full of particles that disperse the light. Because the microscopic dust particles floating in the air scatter blue light more than red and yellow, the sky looks blue.

❧ On February 15, 2009, Texas news stations were inundated with calls and e-mails from viewers witnessing fireballs falling from the sky. Some speculated that the debris was caused by a collision between two satellites earlier that week, but the FAA would not confirm.

❧ In Honduras, the Lluvia de Peces (Rain of Fishes) is a modern-day folklore that has been occurring for more than a century. Witnesses state that it begins with a dark cloud in the sky followed by lightning, thunder, strong winds, and heavy rain for 2 to 3 hours. Once the rain has stopped, hundreds of live, fresh-water fish are found on the ground, which are taken home by the community to cook up. It occurs in the Departamento de Yoro, between the months of May and July.

❧ There are 88 constellations in the sky—most of which can be seen in both the northern and southern hemispheres, depending on the time of year.

❧ An old Scandinavian name for Northern Lights translated to "herring flash," since the lights were believed to be reflections of large swarms of herrings onto the sky.

Sleep

❧ The record for the longest duration without sleep is 18 days, 21 hours, 40 minutes during a rocking chair marathon. The winner reported hallucinations, paranoia, blurred vision, slurred speech and memory, as well as concentration lapses.

❧ It is possible for people to take catnaps with their eyes open and be entirely unaware of it.

❧ If you can fall asleep within less than five minutes of lying down, you may be suffering from sleep deprivation. The average adult human being should fall asleep between 10–15 minutes, suggesting that you're still tired enough to sleep deeply, but not feeling exhausted or sleepy by day.

❧ The continuous brain recordings that led to the discovery of REM (rapid eye-movement) sleep were not done until 1953, partly because the scientists involved were concerned about wasting paper.

❧ Certain types of eye movements during REM sleep correspond to specific movements in dreams indicating that dreaming is not unlike watching a film.

❧ Before Thomas Edison invented the light bulb, people slept approximately 10 hours a night. Today, Americans sleep about 6.9 hours a night during weeknights and 7.5 hours each night on weekends.

❧ Narcoleptics can experience sudden "sleep attacks" that can occur at any moment. The disease is believed to affect 293,000 people in the U.S.

S

Snakes

❧ Snakes have no external ears and use their tongue to channel sound waves.

❧ A snake sleeps with both eyes open.

❧ The Brazilian two-headed blind snake is not actually two-headed, blind, or even an actual snake. It is a lizard that can move backward and forward at will and is the same diameter throughout so its head and tail look the same, hence the "two-headed" moniker.

S

❧ A rattlesnake will die if left in the hot sun for twenty minutes.

❧ Unlike other snakes, the King Cobras will make a nest for its eggs. The female constructs her nest of dead leaves by scooping them up with her large body.

Snuff

🍂 Snuff is a powdered, moist form of tobacco sold in tins. Users apply the snuff between the lower lip or cheek and the gum, or sniff it. The use of snuff is called "dipping."

🍂 Snuff became popular among the English after the looting of a Spanish convoy in Vigo Bay. Among the goods that were taken from the Spanish fleet was a large consignment of snuff, which found its way to London and was brought to ports and coastal towns by discharged sailors who had received it as partial payment of their services and prize money.

🍂 Chew on that…a person who uses 8 to 10 dips or chews a day receives the same amount of nicotine as a heavy smoker who smokes 30 to 40 cigarettes a day.

🍂 From 1702, snuff mills were established in many parts of England, notably in London, Bristol, Sheffield, and Kendal. More than 300 years later, English snuff is still made in Sheffield by Wilson & Co., and in Kendal by Gawith, Hoggarth & Co. and by Samuel Gawith.

🍂 A "snuff bullet" is a snuff container in the shape of a bullet that allows the snuff to be delivered in convenient single shot doses at the turn of a dial. The snuff is then tapped from the bullet and sniffed from the wrist, or the bullet is taken to the nostril and sniffed directly. Snuff Bullets have a little "air hole" in the side that allows for easy sniffing.

S

Soap Bubbles

- Bubbles are made up of molecules that attract each other. This pulls the bubble in, and air pressure inside pushes the bubble out.

- Soap bubbles blown into air that is below 5°F (−15°C) will freeze when they touch a surface. The air inside will gradually diffuse out, causing the bubble to crumple under its own weight.

- Bubbles were used as a toy almost 400 years ago. Children blowing bubbles with clay pipes were depicted in 17th century Flemish paintings.

- U.S. National Bubble Week commences on the first week of spring.

S

- Measuring 156 ft (47.40 m) in length, the world's largest bubble wall was achieved at the Pacific Science Center Seattle Washington on August 11, 1997.

Soccer

❧ The Football Association (FA) was formed in 1862 from the various associations, such as the Sheffield Association or the Nottingham Association, who came together to hold competitions and set out rules for the game. The word "soccer" is an abbreviation of "Association."

❧ In 1314, King Edward II of England disliked soccer so much that he issued a proclamation and anyone playing it would be imprisoned.

❧ Soccer's world governing body, the Federation of International Football Associations, has more members than the United Nations.

❧ Since 1952, Hungary has won the most gold medals in Olympics soccer.

❧ Brazilian soccer player Pelé (Edson Arantes do Nascimento) was the first commercial superstar of soccer and retired as the only player with over 1,000 goals in the sport.

S

Socks

 ❧ The average foot has 250,000 sweat glands, and the average pair of feet releases approximately a half a pint of perspiration each day.

 ❧ Roman comic actors used to wear a type of shoe known as *soccus* in Latin.

 ❧ 40% of the world's socks are made in China.

 ❧ Boys at a Birmingham school in England set a world record for the longest wash line. The line was 1.5 km (nearly a mile!) long and sported 28,400 odd socks. They had assembled 24,500 pegs for their attempt which was aimed to raise money for the schools' charities.

 ❧ During times of wartime shortage, some women would draw a black line up the back of their bare legs to render the seam effect of a stocking.

 ❧ "Sock Hop" was an American term coined in the 50s following the popularity of rock and roll and is associated with informal dances at high schools, typically held at gyms or cafeterias. To avoid damage to the floors, the school directors required kids to remove their shoes before dancing on the floors.

S

Soy

🍂 During the Chou Dynasty (1134–246 BC), the soybean was deemed one of the five sacred grains, along with barley, wheat, millet, and rice.

🍂 More people have soy sauce in their kitchen pantries than tea, coffee, milk, or salsa.

🍂 The *Internet Journal of Toxicology* reported that a Chinese company Hongshuai Soy Sauce marketed their product as "using the latest bioengineering technology." With the prices lower than its competitors' soy sauce, it soon became popular until it was discovered that the company did not use amino acids derived from wheat and soy. The amino acids were derived from human hair swept off barbershop floors.

🍂 In 2009, customs officers seized 250 tins of counterfeit soy sauce valued at more than $60,000 from four wholesalers. Five people—four men and one woman—were arrested. Though no harmful substances were found in the fake soy, the culprits could be subject to a maximum penalty of $500,000 and five years in jail.

🍂 Like other crops such as corn, cotton, and canola, most soybeans in production are genetically modified to improve growing characteristics and yield.

S

SPAM®

 SPAM® was invented in the late Depression and became a godsend during wartime.

 Margaret Thatcher once reported that SPAM® was a "wartime delicacy."

 SPAM® has 174 calories per serving; 137 of those are calories from fat.

 In Korea, SPAM® is made available in nine-can gift boxes. The brand is so popular there that it has spawned imitations including Lo-Spam, Dak, Plumrose, and Tulip, to ensure that no one need go without.

 Hawaiians eat an average of four cans of SPAM® per person per year, more than in any other place on Earth.

S

Speech

🐦 The Karaya Indians of East Brazil are said to speak through their nostrils instead of their lips.

🐦 Men of the Mazateco tribe of Mexico carry out a conversation through the act of whistling, known as the Mazateco whistle speech. Whistle speech can also be found in the occasional European community such as parts of the Canary Islands where on the island of La Gomera, residents communicate by using a language of whistles that can take over five years to learn.

🐦 The Zulus of South Africa speak a language that includes fifteen different clicking sounds as consonants.

🐦 A human being requires about 100 muscles of the chest, neck, jaw, tongue and lips to produce one phrase.

🐦 The average English conversation operates at about 150 words per minute.

S

Spice

- The average American consumes about 4500mg of salt per day, which is equivalent to about 2 teaspoons. The body only requires about 200mg.

- The Cinnamon Bird is a legendary Arabian bird that used cinnamon to build its nests. Herodotus wrote that these birds flew to a foreign land to gather the cinnamon and brought it back with them to Arabia. The Arabians, in turn, got the cinnamon by tempting the birds with large chunks of raw meat. When the birds brought the meat back to their nests, the weight caused the nests to fall and be collected by the people.

- In traditional herb gardens, rosemary was commonly associated with lavender, both of which belong to the mint family.

S

- The term mustard comes from the Latin words *mustum ardens*, which translates to "burning wine." It refers to the taste created by the heat of the crushed mustard seeds mixed with the juice of unfermented wine grapes.

- To prolong basil storage, freeze chopped basil and olive oil in plastic ice cubes or very small freezer containers. Use them as needed.

- In ancient times, corpses were sprinkled with parsley to help remove the stench. In current times, parsley can be used to freshen breath.

Stamps

⚜ The country of Bhutan issued a group of postage stamps in 1973 that were actually phonograph records. These stamps had native folk songs recorded on one side that could be played on a record player.

⚜ Around 1883, the U.S. witnessed early forms of product placement in the form of a stamp. Advertising for various products was printed on the back of three-cent stamps.

⚜ During the Apollo 11 moon flight in 1969, the astronauts had a die of a postage stamp, which they pulled an impression of when they touched down on the moon. Once the die was returned to earth, it was used to produce the 10-cent airmail stamp issued in September of 1969. Truly a stamp that was out of this world.

⚜ As the first country to issue stamps, Britain is the only country to have stamps without its name printed on it.

⚜ The most popular U.S. postage stamp sold over 120 million copies. It was a 1993 stamp of rock singer Elvis Presley.

⚜ "Black on Magenta," the 1856 1 cent British Guiana stamp, is the most rare and expensive stamp in the world. It is valued at $3 million today, but it hasn't been sold since 1980 when it went for $1 million.

S

Star Wars

🐌 Harrison Ford was fitting a door for Francis Ford Coppola when a studio exec asked him to take a break to read some lines with actresses who were testing the film. The force was with him to land the role of Han Solo.

🐌 Sir Alec Guinness, who played Ben "Obi-Wan" Kenobi in the film, made a fortune. He had negotiated a deal for 2% of the box office revenue.

🐌 George Lucas had planned to have the film score sound like the classical music in Stanley Kubrick's *2001: A Space Odyssey* before Steven Spielberg introduced him to composer John Williams.

🐌 When writing the script, George Lucas briefly considered making the characters of Luke Skywalker and his aunt and uncle dwarves.

🐌 George Lucas's friend Francis Ford Coppola was the inspiration for the character of Han Solo.

🐌 In Italy, Darth Vader was known as "Dart Fener," because the word "Vader" sounds too close to the Italian word for the toilet bowl.

🐌 George Lucas once said that the Millenium Falcon's shape was modeled after a hamburger.

S

Star-Spangled Banner

❧ "The Star-Spangled Banner," was a poem written by Francis Scott Key in 1814. He set the words to a popular British drinking song, "To Anacreon in Heaven."

❧ In 1916, President Woodrow Wilson stated that the "Banner" should be played by the military and naval services.

❧ On March 3, 1931, the "Banner" was officially announced as the national anthem by an act of Congress.

❧ The song's first performance at a sporting event was at the 1918 World Series.

❧ Jimi Hendrix's solo guitar performance of the song at the 1969 Woodstock Festival was one of the most controversial renditions. He played the anthem with a number of distorted regressions using mimicking planes, bombs, and screams in reference to the Vietnam War. *Guitar World* magazine voted it as 52nd on the list of the 100 greatest guitar solos of all time.

S

Statue of Liberty

- The face on the Statue of Liberty measures more than 8 ft tall.

- Heavy metal…the statue has seven rays on her crown, one for each of the seven continents, and with each measuring up to 9 ft in length and weighing as much as 150 lbs.

- The tablet held in her left hand is inscribed with the date America declared her independence: JULY IV MDCCLXXVI or July 4, 1776.

- The statue, designed by Frenchman Auguste Bartholdi, was assembled twice. After designing smaller scale working models, the designer and his crew constructed the full-size statue in Paris. Once fully built, the statue was disassembled, packed up, and sent across the Atlantic for re-assembly.

- Copper develops its blue-green patina as a result of exposure to air and to reduce further oxidation. Studies have revealed that only the top 5% of the statue's skin has oxidized in the first 100 years.

S

Sting

❧ The nickname "Sting" was coined for artist Gordon Sumner because he used to don a black and yellow striped sweater while performing.

❧ The rock-reggae smash-hit "Roxanne," catapulted to the top of the charts after it was banned from the BBC.

❧ In March 1980, the Police embarked on their first world tour and were one of the first global rock bands to tour Bombay, India and Egypt.

❧ As of 2003, Sting was still reeling in an average of $2000 per day in royalties for the over 20-year-old song "Every Breath You Take."

❧ Dennis Wilson, former Beach Boys drummer, stated that "Every Breath You Take" was his favorite song of all time and had it played at his funeral in 1983.

S

Sugar

🌿 The name originates from the Sanskrit word for *Sharkara*, which means "material in a granule form."

🌿 Until the late 18th century, sugar was considered a luxury item that European nobility used to confirm their rank and social power. It was known as "White Gold."

🌿 A spoonful of sugar added to a vase of water will prolong the life of freshly cut flowers.

🌿 During World War II, people were only allowed 4 oz sugar a week as part of their rations.

S

🌿 Adding three or four sugar cubes to a suitcase before storage will help prevent musty odors.

Sun

🐦 The Sun is comprised of various elements. 74% of its mass comes from hydrogen, 24% helium, and the remaining 2% includes trace amounts of iron, nickel, oxygen, and all the other elements in the Solar System.

🐦 Each day, 4.5 lbs of sunlight strike the earth.

🐦 The sun is held together by gravity.

🐦 Sunspots, the dark spots on the surface of the Sun, are magnetic regions with a magnetic field strength that is thousands of times stronger than the Earth's.

🐦 Because the Sun is a giant sphere of hydrogen gas, different parts of the Sun rotate at different speeds. The speed at which the surface rotates can be tracked by the movements of the sunspots across the surface. Regions at the equator take 25 days to complete one rotation, while features at the poles can take 36 days.

S

Surfing

🏄 Big wave surfing is a style of surfing where surfers paddle into—or are towed onto—waves which are at least 20 ft high. With bigger waves, there is a need for bigger boards called "guns" or "rhino chasers."

🏄 Do you know your surf ABCs? Surfing is so popular that it has its own dedicated lexicon. An "Acid Drop" is when you take off on a wave, then have the bottom suddenly fall out, so you free fall down the face. "Brosef" is a higher rank than "brah" (brother), or someone who has earned one's profound respect. "Cactus Juiced" is a type of injury, which leaves the surfer unable to surf.

🏄 Mavericks is an area of beach in San Mateo County, CA, considered to be one of the three best surfing locations in the world. Winter storms can create waves of up to 30 ft.

🏄 In the 1987 pseudo-surf B-movie entitled *North Shore*, real-life surf champion (and brosef?) Laird Hamilton played the violent, antagonistic thug-surfer role of "Lance Burkhart."

🏄 The University of Plymouth in England offers a BSc (Hons) in Surf Science & Technology. The program is centered around coastal/ocean sciences, surfing equipment/clothing design, and surfing-related business.

S

Taj Mahal

❧ When emperor Shan Hahan lost his third wife and the love of his life, Mumtaz Mahal, he vowed to construct the most beautiful monument in her honour. He commissioned the leading designer at the time, Ustad Ahmad Lahauri, to build it and thus the Taj Mahal was born.

❧ More than 1,000 elephants were used for the transportation of the construction materials.

❧ 28 different varieties of semi-precious and precious stones were used to embellish the Taj with ornate inlay work.

❧ The entire design of the Taj Mahal is completely symmetrical with four minarets, at each corner of the plinth surrounding the tomb.

❧ The sides of Mumtaz Mahal's tomb have calligraphic inscriptions featuring ninety-nine names of God.

❧ During the Indian uprising of 1857, the Taj Mahal was defaced by the British who plucked precious stones from its walls.

❧ The mausoleum took 22 years to complete with a workforce of 20,000 people. Craftsmen from as far as Turkey were commissioned to work.

T

Taxes

~❧ Both ancient Greece and Rome levied taxes on consumption, but to maximize revenues, the state collected taxes on imported goods rather than taxing its citizens directly. Julius Caesar introduced a sales tax of 1%, and prior to that, there was a 5% inheritance tax in Rome.

~❧ In 1695, American colonies levied a tax on bachelors to encourage young men to marry.

~❧ In 1799, Prime Minister William Pitt the Younger imposed Income Tax at a rate of 2.5% to fund the Napoleonic War—it was also planned to be temporary.

~❧ In Tennessee, one has 48 hours to report acquisitions of illegal drugs (even moonshine) to the Department of Revenue to pay tax. In exchange, a stamp will be affixed to the illegal substance to prove that a tax has been paid.

~❧ Since 2004, Maryland levies a tax on homeowners and businesses for producing wastewater. The money goes toward protecting the Chesapeake Bay waters. Virginia also had plans to instate a flush tax of $1 a week per household.

~❧ In 1916, Congress deleted the word "lawful" before the word "income" in order to tax illegal income.

Tea

❧ Outside of China, Arabs were the first to mention tea in 850 AD.

❧ Struggling to cut costs, a New York coffee merchant named Thomas Sullivan turned to tea and began sending out samples of it in silk muslin bags. His idea was misinterpreted so recipients used them as tea bags. The idea eventually caught on.

❧ Tea reached England in the 1600s but because it was shipped from China and took between 12–16 months to arrive, only members of the royalty or aristocracy could afford it.

❧ In some regions around the world, such as Tibet, Mongolia and parts of China, people take their tea with salt rather than sugar.

❧ 80% of tea sold in the U.S. is iced tea.

T

Tennis

꙳ In the 11th century, French monks began playing a game around the monastery using a crude handball and a rope strung across the courtyard. As the game evolved, it became popular with royalty before catching on in England by the 13th century. When returning a ball over the net, the French players shouted *tenez* meaning "here it comes" or "take it."

꙳ The tennis ball is only in play for about twenty minutes during a two and a half hour match.

꙳ Tiffany & Co makes the U.S. Open Trophy. In case you were wondering, it is not made available through the wedding registry.

꙳ "Love" is the word used when the score is zero, or goose egg, because it originally sounded like the French word for egg, *l'oeuf.*

꙳ Women on top! Martina Navratilova has won nine Wimbledon singles titles. She also tied Billie Jean King's record number of 20 Wimbledon titles.

Tesla, Nikola

🕊 Nikola Tesla, a prominent inventor and mechanical and electrical engineer, received over 800 different patents, and scientists continue to scour through his notes today. He's been referred to as "the man who invented the 20th century."

🕊 Tesla claimed to sleep only 2 to 3 hours a day whereas Sir Isaac Newton needed 3 to 4 hours daily.

🕊 Current affairs…at the 1893 World Exposition in Chicago, Tesla demonstrated how safe AC electricity was by passing the high frequency power through his body to power light bulbs. He was then able to shoot large lightning bolts from his Tesla coils to the crowd without harm.

🕊 When Tesla arrived in the United States in 1884 to work for Thomas Edison's company, one of his first assignments was to redesign the company's direct current generators. Edison reportedly agreed to pay Tesla $50,000 but reneged on the offer when Tesla proved the modifications were successful. Tesla resigned shortly thereafter.

🕊 In 1910, Tesla began to demonstrate obvious symptoms of obsessive-compulsive order. He was obsessed with the number three and often walked around a building three times before entering and demanded a stack of three folded napkins next to him at each meal.

🕊 David Bowie initially turned down the part of Tesla in the film, *The Prestige*, but Christopher Nolan, a lifelong fan of Bowie's, flew to New York to pitch the role in person.

T

Testosterone

꙳ Testosterone, which is produced by the testicles, is linked to sexual function, memory, concentration, and mood. When the hormone is low, a man may demonstrate lethargy, irritability, and a smaller libido.

꙳ For athletes, the hormone affects everything from muscle size, strength, and the size of the heart to the amount of oxygen-carrying blood cells in the body and the percentage of fat on the body.

꙳ Testosterone is known as the "male hormone," but women produce small amounts throughout their lives—approximately one-seventh the amount per day that men make.

꙳ The amount of testosterone produced in the body will decrease naturally with age. It begins around the age of 25, sometimes decreasing as much as 10% per decade.

꙳ Scientists have stated that there is evidence that saliva has testosterone in it and that the act of kissing may be linked with an increase in sex drive.

T

Thanksgiving

🐦 The initial hunting party for the first Thanksgiving feast was also a fishing party where lobsters, bass, and clams were on the menu.

🐦 Very few people know that the first U.S. Thanksgiving celebrated by colonists did not take place in Plymouth, MA. On December 3, 1619, the first Thanksgiving feast was held at Berkeley Hundred, a tobacco plantation near Jamestown, VA. Thirty-eight men landed here and held a Thanksgiving Day celebration nearly a year before the pilgrims settled on Plymouth Rock.

🐦 In the 19th century, Sarah Josepha Hale, an influential magazine editor and author, launched a campaign to make Thanksgiving a national holiday. She was also the author of the classic nursery rhyme "Mary Had a Little Lamb."

🐦 According to the National Turkey Federation, an estimated 46 million turkeys in 2007 were eaten at Thanksgiving. This made up one-fifth of the total turkeys consumed that year.

T

Tiger

 A tiger's roar can be heard from two miles away.

 At one time, there were eight tiger subspecies roaming the Earth. Today, there are only five left.

 She's a man-eater...the Champawat Tigress is thought to have killed over 430 people in India decades ago until famous hunter Jim Corbett finally killed her.

 The heaviest recorded tiger was a Siberian that tipped the scales at 1,025 lbs.

T All tigers share similar markings on their forehead, which resembles the Chinese symbol *Wang*, meaning "King."

Time

❧ At the end of 1982, the personal computer was selected as *Time* magazine's "Man of the Year."

❧ In 2007, the year's first issue was delayed by a week due to "editorial changes" that happened to include the job losses of 49 employees.

❧ *Time* introduced its signature red border in 1927 and has only changed it twice since the first issue. The issue released shortly after 9/11 featured a black border to symbolize mourning. Its April 28, 2008 Earth Day issue featured a green border.

❧ On September 10, 2007, *Time* was ordered to pay $106 million in defamation damages to former Indonesian President Suharto. They had published a May 1999 cover story alleging Suharto and his family had amassed a fortune of around $15 billion, including $9 billion in an Austrian bank account. Despite the order to pay, they have always stood by their story.

❧ In 2009, *Time* created a list of the 25 people to blame for the financial crisis. Topping the list is Angelo Mozilo, formerly the chairman of the board and chief executive officer of Countrywide Financial until July 1, 2008. The CEO helped cause the US massive mortgage crisis by providing loans to people who could never afford to pay them back.

T

Titanic

- The passengers on the ship had a wealth of luxuries at their disposable, many of which were a first on a ship. A heated swimming pool, Turkish bath, squash court, gymnasium, and libraries were just some of the amenities for the guests. Each of the 840 staterooms also had electric lighting and heating, which was a luxury in 1912.

- The band was playing "Nearer My God To Thee" as the ship was sinking.

- The seawater was around 28°F (−2°C) on the night it sank.

- James Cameron first shot footage of the real wreck of the *Titanic* in 1995 and used that to convince 20th Century Fox to invest in the film, persuading them that the publicity surrounding a real-life dive to the wreck would benefit the production.

- The film had a record $200,000,000 budget at the time, which cost more than the *Titanic* itself. The cost to construct the ship between 1910–1912 was around $7.5 million at the time and about $120 to $150 million in 1997 dollars.

Toast

🐦 The process that caramelizes the bread, cooking the sugar and turning it golden brown, begins at 310°F and is known as the Maillard reaction. This reaction gives the flavor and crunch to toast.

🐦 "El Tosto," the first electric toaster, was most likely invented in 1905, when inventor Albert Marsh developed the Nichrome wire, making the electric toaster possible.

🐦 The first automated pop-up toaster was invented in 1926 and went for a staggering $150 by today's standards.

🐦 The Smithsonian's National Museum of American History boasts a collection of nearly 100 non-electric and electric toasters, ranging from the 18th century to the 1980s.

🐦 French toast is also known as "Eggy Bread" in the UK, *pain perdu* in French, or *pain doré* in French-speaking parts of Canada.

🐦 Sanrio offers a Hello Kitty toaster in its collection of products. Each piece of toast is embedded with Kitty's whiskered face on every slice of bread.

Tobacco

- In 1557, European doctors recommended smoking to fight bad breath and cancer.

- Sir Francis Bacon, creator of the scientific method, admitted that it was difficult to quit smoking in 1610.

- In 1776, Americans used tobacco as collateral for French loans to subsidize payment for the American Revolution.

- Phillip Morris's cigarette mascot was once a tattooed sailor before changing to the Marlboro Man in 1963.

- Invented in England in 1774, the tobacco resuscitation kit was used to revive victims of drowning, by introducing warmth and stimulation to the "apparently dead" victim. Bellows were used to inject tobacco smoke up the rectum, or into the lungs through the mouth and nose.

- The use of tobacco products does not only lead to a number of health problems and diseases, but smokers can also develop bad breath, black hairy tongues, ground-down teeth, and receding gums.

Toilet Paper

- The standard size of a sheet of toilet paper is 4.5 in × 4.5 in.

- 1-ply toilet paper is generally cheaper and more economical to use as people use the same amount of sheets regardless of plies.

- In 1996, President Clinton levied a tax on toilet paper. Each roll was taxed 6 cents and increased the price of the product to 30 cents per roll.

- The fiber (bast) and pulp (hurd) of the hemp plant can be used to manufacture toilet paper and is made free of chemicals.

- Prior to the advent of toilet paper, a variety of different wipes were used. Newsprint and paper catalogues were used in the U.S.; discarded sheep's wool during the Viking Age in England; frayed ends of old anchor cables were used by sailing crews from Spain and Portugal; lace was used by French Royalty; and snow or tundra moss by early Eskimos.

- In the early 20th century, manufacturers looked for angles to market toilet paper. Scott advertisements stated that "over 65% of middle-aged men and women suffered from some sort of rectal disease" and that using inferior toilet paper was consequential to one's well being because "harsh toilet tissue may cause serious injury."

T

Tomatoes

🍂 There are more than 10,000 varieties of tomatoes.

🍂 Tomato juice is the official state beverage of Ohio, while the vine-ripe pink tomato is Arkansas' official state vegetable.

🍂 Tomatoes should never be refrigerated as the cold causes them to lose their nutritional value and flavor. Tomatoes are best stored above 55°F (around 12°C).

🍂 You say tomato…a fruit is any fleshy material covering a seed or seeds so botanically speaking, the tomato is a fruit. From a horticultural aspect, though, it is considered a vegetable because it is an annual and non-woody.

🍂 The word tomato comes from the Nuhautl word, *tomatl*. The language is indigenous to central Mexico.

🍂 Tomatoes are high in Lycopene, an antioxidant that helps protect against cancer.

T

Tornado

❧ The funnel-shaped whirling winds that make up a tornado can reach a speed of 300mph.

❧ Though they can potentially move in any direction, the average tornado moves southwest to northeast.

❧ According to FEMA (Federal Emergency Management Agency), if you're outside and without shelter, the best way to protect yourself is to lie flat in a nearby ditch or depression and cover your head with your hands. Also, pay close attention to potential flooding.

T

❧ The funnel clouds generally last less than ten minutes before dissipating. Occasionally, the cyclones can last for more than an hour, as reported in the early twentieth century.

❧ In the U.S., May is the most popular month for tornadoes with an average of 176 each year between 1950 and 1999. However, April has the most fatalities with an average of 26 tornado-related deaths over that time period.

❧ Tornado Alley is a flat stretch of land between west Texas and North Dakota. This is a prime region for tornadoes as the dry polar air from Canada meets the warm tropical air from the Gulf of Mexico.

Trains

～ With a gradient of 48%, the steepest Cogwheel railway in the world is in Switzerland.

～ Skunk Trains are vintage locomotives that were first designed with gasoline engines (they run on diesel today), and used a potbelly stove for heating. The smell would drift into town on the breeze and locals would call out, "You can smell 'em before you can see 'em!!" Hence the name.

～ The single longest journey on one train can be taken on the Trans-Siberian Express between Moscow and Vladivostok in Russia.

～ According to the official Amtrak Web site, Amtrak is short for "American Track."

～ The Huey Long Bridge over the Mississippi River just above New Orleans is the longest railway-highway bridge of steel and concrete in the U.S. It is 4.4 miles in length, including approaches.

T

Trump, Donald

❧ Donald Trump does not smoke or drink alcohol and has a terrible fear of baldness and of disease.

❧ He was voted "Ladies' Man" by classmates of New York Military Academy's class of 1964 at Cornwall-on-Hudson, NY.

❧ He is a longtime fan of wrestling and close friends with wrestling personality, Vince McMahon. Trump hosted Wrestlemania IV and V at Trump Plaza, and appeared in a ringside seat at a few others.

❧ Trump declared bankruptcy in 1990 and has built his fortune since. In fact, he is currently thought to be worth around $1.6 billion.

❧ Many developers pay Donald Trump to license his name on projects; therefore, Trump does not own many of the buildings that feature his name. According to *Forbes*, this portion of Trump's empire is run by his children and the most valuable by far, at $562 million.

T

Turner, Tina

- Tina Turner was born Anna Mae Bullock to a mixed race couple. When Tina was just 10, her mother abandoned both her and her sister. At 13, her father left them too. She was raised by her grandmother and extended family.

- Tina has sold more concert tickets than any other solo performer in the history of music.

- The constant abuse by Ike Turner during their marriage forced Tina to have reconstructive surgery to her nose.

- In 2001, the Tina Turner Highway became part of the Tennessee State Route 19 between Brownsville and Nutbush.

- In the film *Mad Max Beyond Thunderdome*, the character Aunt Entity was scripted to drive. Unfortunately, all the cars were stick shifts, which Tina couldn't drive, so a special automatic vehicle was constructed for her.

- In the film biopic *What's Love Got to Do with It*, both Angela Bassett and Laurence Fishburne were nominated for Oscars for their roles depicting Tina Turner and Ike Turner.

T

Turtles and Tortoises

❧ At top speed, a giant tortoise can only manage to travel at about five yards a minute, or .17mph.

❧ The Kemp's Ridley turtle is the smallest, rarest sea turtle. They are so protected that the Mexican government sends Marines to guard the only beach on which they lay their eggs.

❧ In warm summer water, the average turtle's heart will beat up to 40 times a minute; whereas in winter when the water is cold, the turtle's heart beats only once every ten minutes.

❧ A desert tortoise can survive an entire year on what a cow eats in one day.

❧ Turtles and tortoises are unlike any other vertebrates because their hipbones and shoulder bones are *inside* their rib cage.

❧ The Wood Turtle emits a courting whistle which sounds like a teakettle. It can be heard 40 ft away.

T

Twain, Mark

🐦 "Always acknowledge a fault. This will throw those in authority off their guard and give you an opportunity to commit more."—Mark Twain

🐦 Mark Twain's real name was Samuel Langhorne Clemens. Twain got the idea for the name after hearing the leadsman on the paddle steamers calling out "mark twain" to indicate the depth of the river. "Mark" described the knots and "twain" is an old-fashioned way of saying "two" and a fathom is six ft.

🐦 To pay off accrued debts from failed business investments, Twain traveled the world as a lecturer and published his experiences in *Following the Equator.*

🐦 Before he became Mark Twain, he wrote under the pen name "Thomas Jefferson Snodgrass" for three humorous pieces he contributed to the *Keokuk Post.*

🐦 The American Library Association ranked *Huckleberry Finn* as the fifth most frequently challenged book in the United States.

🐦 Twain loved cats. When he was older and summering in New Hampshire, he would rent kittens from a nearby farm to have as companions until he returned home.

T

Twix®

🍂 First introduced in 1979, the Twix® candy bar was known as a "Raider" bar in France and Germany until Mars decided to standardize the name in 1991.

🍂 Peanut Butter Twix® was available in North America from 1983 to 1997, and made a permanent return in 2000. The peanut butter replaces the caramel in this version.

🍂 Introduced in 2005, the White Chocolate Twix® was available in Australia, Ireland, and the UK. White Twix® is currently available in the United States as a limited edition.

🍂 200 calories of Twix® Cookie Bars can be burned off with a mere 30 minutes of swimming, 18 minutes of running, 22 minutes of cross-training, or 38 minutes of bicycling.

🍂 As of 2007, Mars announced that Twix® bars in Europe are no longer vegetarian. The whey in Twix®—as well as Celebrations, Bounty, and the Milky Way bar—are still made from animal rennet.

T

Uganda

- Half the population of Uganda is under the age of 15. In 2008, the estimated life expectancy of a citizen in Uganda was only 52.

- Almost half of the world's remaining mountain gorillas live in the Virunga Mountains of central Africa, where Uganda, Rwanda, and the Democratic Republic of the Congo intersect.

- English became the official language of Uganda after independence, but there are nearly forty different languages that are regularly and currently in use in the country.

- *Matoke*, the Ugandan plantain or banana, is a staple crop in the country. The bananas are often wrapped in plantain leaves and steamed until tender and then served with or without meat.

- Uganda will only accept foreign U.S. dollar bills that are printed on and after 2001. In addition, they must be in good condition, not torn and preferably in large denominations of the new style bills. Many bureaus refuse the old bills because they're considered suspect.

- Grassroots organizations are raising awareness about the children who were kidnapped by the Lord's Resistance Army and exploited as young soldiers or wives. Thousands of children as young as eight were captured and forced to kill. The film *Invisible Children* documents the tragic lives of the children, known as night commuters, who fled their villages at night to avoid abduction.

Ukulele

🐦 The word "ukulele" is a rough translation of the Hawaiian word for "jumping flea."

🐦 Though the ukulele is most commonly linked with Hawaii, the instrument was derived from two different Portuguese instruments: the braguinha and the cavaquinho.

🐦 With new strings, the ukulele will not hold a tune for more than a few seconds, because the strings require up to two weeks to stretch out. So if you should ever play out of tune, just blame it on the strings.

🐦 In the film *Fifty First Dates*, actor Adam Sandler played a custom 6-string Kamaka ukulele designed to his specifications. The instrument appears in the movie's official poster and on the cover of the DVD and soundtrack, although the ukulele was digitally modified to resemble a 4-string.

🐦 The late musician George Harrison, who was known primarily as a guitarist, was a huge fan of the ukulele and would take one wherever he went. According to a store in Maui, Harrison bought out all the ukuleles in stock to give as gifts to friends.

U

United Nations

❧ On October 24, 1945, the United Nations officially came into existence when its Charter was given consent by the five permanent members of the Security Council (France, the Republic of China, the Soviet Union, the United Kingdom and the United States) as well as a majority of 46 other member countries.

❧ A different type of toilet humor...President Franklin Roosevelt pitched the name "United Nations" to Winston Churchill back in 1942. At the time, Churchill was in Washington, DC, sitting in the bathtub when Roosevelt was wheeled into the bathroom with his pitch. They both thought the name sounded better than "Alliance," a name they were first considering.

❧ The UN Headquarters building in New York City was designed by Le Corbusier and Oscar Niemeyer, and built with an interest-free loan from the U.S.

❧ Even though the land and the building of the UN Headquarters is in New York City, the area is considered international territory so it doesn't necessarily need to meet all of the city's fire safety and building codes.

❧ The United Nations has its own post office and its own postage stamp, though the stamp is mostly used as a collectible.

❧ In 2006, Montenegro became the 192nd member of the United Nations. In addition to the member states, there is one non-member observer state: Holy See in Vatican City.

U

Uranus

🕊 Uranus is very cold. Unlike other large planets in the solar system, it emits less heat than it absorbs from the sun. The temperature is about −355°F (−215°C).

🕊 True blue…The methane in Uranus's atmosphere filters out the color red which is what cause its pale blue appearance.

🕊 In Greek mythology, Uranus was the god of the skies and husband of Earth.

🕊 Uranus has a 17-hour day, but the tilt of the planet is designed so that only one pole faces the Sun. In fact, a day at the north pole will last half a Uranian year, or 84 Earth years.

🕊 Uranus can be seen without a telescope…at magnitude 5.3, the planet is just within the brightness range that a human eye can perceive. To see it, all you need is a pair of binoculars and some very dark skies.

U

Utah

❧ Feet first! Utah boasts the largest dinosaur footprints. The prints belonged to a hadrosaurid (duckbill).

❧ Great Salt Lake is several times saltier than seawater. It is so salty that swimmers float above the water.

❧ The federal government owns 60% of Utah's land.

U

❧ About 70% of Utahans are members of the Church of Jesus Christ of Latter-day Saints, which has its headquarters in Salt Lake City.

❧ The name "Utah" comes from the Native American *Ute* tribe and translates as "people of the mountains."

Valentine's Day

In 270 AD, Roman emperor Claudius II believed married men were bad soldiers and decreed that all young men were barred from marriage. Ignoring the emperor, Bishop Valentine continued to marry young lovers in secret until his disobedience was discovered, and he was sentenced to death.

Saint Valentine's Day is still celebrated in the same fashion today as it was in the 14th century.

In Minsk, Belorussia, 6,000 people participated in a simultaneous Valentine's Day kiss.

In Japan and Korea, it has become a near obligation for women to give chocolates, known as *giri-choco*, to all of their co-workers on Valentine's Day.

The first Valentine's Day card was sent in 1415. While imprisoned in the Tower of London following the Battle of Agincourt, France's Duke of Orléans sent one to his beloved wife.

Vatican

✎ Vatican City may be the world's smallest independent nation, but it is the spiritual capital for the world's one billion Catholics.

✎ Almost all of Vatican City's 890 citizens live inside the Vatican's walls. The citizens include high-ranking dignitaries, priests, nuns, guards, as well as about 3,000 lay workers.

✎ "Holy See" is a term used to describe the composite of the authority, jurisdiction, and sovereignty vested in the Pope and his advisers to direct the worldwide Roman Catholic Church. The Holy See is the "central government" of the Roman Catholic Church and has legal authority to enter into treaties as the juridical equivalent of a state.

✎ Vatican City has a press that can print books or pamphlets in any language, from Old Ecclesiastical Georgian to the Tamil language of India and Sri Lanka.

✎ Vatican City gained independence from Italy on February 11, 1929.

Vaudeville

❧ Similar to the English music hall, American vaudeville was a stage entertainment consisting of unrelated songs, dances, acrobatic and magic acts, as well as humorous skits and sketches. It branched out further to include the concert saloon, minstrelsy, freak shows, dime museums, and literary burlesque.

❧ There are a few theories about the origination of the word "vaudeville," but one of the explanations is that it is a derivation from the French expression *voix de ville*, or "voice of the city."

❧ Palace Theatre, the most prominent vaudeville venue of its time, was built by California vaudeville entrepreneur Martin Beck, who created the Palace to be the 'Valhalla of Vaudeville."

❧ Famed acts including the Three Stooges, Abbott and Costello, Kate Smith, Bob Hope, Judy Garland, and Rose Marie all used vaudeville purely as launching pads for later careers, leaving live performance before they had ever risen to their respective heights of fame.

❧ For years, Harry Houdini was the highest grossing performer in vaudeville.

V

Vegetables

- Carrots, as most of us know, are orange. However, carrots come in a spectrum of colors such as purple, red, yellow, and even white.

- In Europe, the eggplant—also known as aubergine—was once thought to cause insanity and was known as the Mad Apple.

- The word broccoli is derived from *brachium*, the Latin word for "arm". It is a good source of Vitamin A and C, potassium, folacin, iron, and fiber.

- The ancient Egyptians worshipped the onion, and believed that the spherical shape and concentric rings embodied eternity. The onion was the only vegetable at the time to be crafted out of gold by Egyptian artists.

- In 1995, potatoes were taken into space aboard the shuttle Columbia, which marked the first time food had been grown in space.

V

Venice

❧ The "official" birth date of Venice is March 25, 421 when the city was built upon a salty marshland at the mouth of the Adriatic Sea.

❧ Built on an archipelago of 118 islands, Venice has 150 canals connected by 409 bridges and over 3000 alleyways.

❧ Venice's population has halved over the last fifty years and is currently estimated at about 63,000. The relocation is due in large part to the high living costs and the inconvenience of living away from the mainland. Tourists, in fact, outnumber residents 2 to 1.

❧ There is no sewer system in Venice. All household waste flows into the canals and flushes out into the ocean twice a day with the tides.

❧ Venetian masks are a centuries-old pastime of Venice, Italy. In the past, they were occasionally used to disguise people's identity and social status.

❧ For years, Venice's land has been sinking while the surrounding sea has been rising due to climate change. Unless action is taken, it's possible that Venice will be uninhabitable by the year 2100.

V

Venus

- Double time...Venus and Earth are so similar in size that they are considered twins.

- Venus is the brightest planet and star in the sky.

- The temperature of the surface of Venus scorches at 870°F (466°C). This is higher than any other planet and hotter than most ovens; no animal on Earth could survive the conditions.

- Venus rotates very slowly: one day in Venus is equivalent to 243 Earth days.

- The planet also rotates backwards, unlike any other planet in the solar system.

- Venus has no moons.

V

Vespa®

🐚 Vespa®, an Italian line of scooters manufactured by Piaggio, is now Europe's largest manufacturer of two-wheeled vehicles, and the world's fourth largest motorcycle manufacturer by unit sales. The inspiration for the original classic scooter was derived from the pre-WWII Cushman scooters which were made in Nebraska and exported to Italy in large numbers.

🐚 If Americans were to switch just 10% of their total mileage to scooters, they would consume 14 million gallons less fuel and reduce CO_2 emissions by 324 million pounds in just one day.

🐚 Buzz worthy…Vespa is the Italian word for wasp. When examining the prototype with its wide seated central part and the narrow waist, the founder exclaimed, "It looks like a wasp!"

🐚 Vespa® scooters were a stylish and economical mode of transportation for Mods in the late 1950s to mid 1960s.

🐚 Hollywood greatly influenced the sale of Vespas® during the height of their popularity. Audrey Hepburn and Gregory Peck cruised around Rome on a Vespa® in *Roman Holiday*, which resulted in huge sales increases.

V

Vienna

❧ Vienna is thought to be the birthplace of modern zoo keeping. The zoo at Tiergarten Schonbrun was commissioned by the Empress Maria Theresa and her husband Franz Stephan (who later became Holy Roman Emperor Francis I). In 1778, the zoo opened its doors to the public on Sundays only and to "decently dressed persons."

❧ The city center in Vienna is a World Heritage Site. In 2005, an Economist Intelligence unit study of 127 world cities ranked Vienna first for quality of life...alongside Vancouver, Canada.

❧ Dancing divas...Vienna is the last-standing capital of the nineteenth century ball. More than 200 significant balls are held annually, some of which feature as many as nine live orchestras. The balls generally begin at 9pm and can go on until 5am.

❧ Vienna was home to many influential artists and world-renowned personalities including painter Gustav Klimt, Sigmund Freud, author Arthur Schnitzler, Wolfgang Amadeus Mozart, Ludwig van Beethoven, Johann Strauß, and Gustav Mahler.

❧ Local culinary delights include Wiener Schnitzel, Knödel (dumplings), and decadent desserts such as the Sachertorte, which is Vienna's most famed chocolate cake.

Volcanoes

❧ The name "volcano" is derived from the name of Vulcan, the Roman god of fire.

❧ Mount Erubus is an active volcano in Antarctica that spews pieces of pure gold when it erupts. In this region, all that glitters really *is* gold.

❧ Scientists discovered a volcano in the Bismarck Sea off the coast of Papua New Guinea. It emits molten gold and silver.

❧ In 1994, scientists discovered a volcano near the South Pole under 1.2 miles of ice.

❧ Active volcanoes in the U.S. can be found in Hawaii, Alaska, California, Oregon and Washington; however, Hawaii and Alaska are the only two states with the greatest chance of eruption near communities.

V

Waldorf Astoria

🐦 The Waldorf Astoria Hotel, the famed luxury hotel in New York City, first started as two hotels—one owned by William Waldorf Astor and the other owned by his cousin, John Jacob Astor IV.

🐦 The Waldorf Astoria was the first hotel to abolish the "ladies" entrance as well as the first to serve room service.

🐦 Star power…famous residents have included Marilyn Monroe, Cole Porter, Bugsy Siegel, and Nikola Tesla.

🐦 The *Titanic* hearings were conducted by a special subcommittee of the Senate Commerce Committee and chaired by Senator William A. Smith. These hearings were held at the original Waldorf Astoria.

🐦 It is the only hotel in the world to be home to an official Embassy—the residence of the U.S. Embassy to the United Nations.

🐦 The hotel boasts an international staff that can interpret and translate most languages in the world.

🐦 The Waldorf Astoria and Waldorf Towers offers a total of 1,416 guest rooms and suites, featuring original Art Deco motifs. Each room is decorated differently; no two are exactly alike.

Walrus

❧ Found near the Arctic Circle, the moustached and long-tusked walruses are extremely sociable, prone to bellowing and snorting at each other. But when push comes to shove, these marina mammals become more aggressive during mating season.

❧ In the 18th and 19th centuries, walrus tusks, oil, skin, and meat were in such high demand that they were hunted to extinction in the Gulf of St. Lawrence and around Sable Island, off the coast of Nova Scotia. Today, only Native Americans are allowed to hunt walruses.

❧ These tusks weren't made for walking…Walrus tusks are designed to help the blubbery animals haul themselves out of water.

❧ Walruses can weigh up to 1.5 tons, and their blubber insulates them from the cold and can be up to 15 cm thick.

❧ Don't let its size deceive you. Walruses are natural swimmers that can reach speeds of up to 35 km/hr.

W

Warhol, Andy

- "The idea is not to live forever, it is to create something that will."—Andy Warhol

- Andy's brother, Paul Warhol, featured an exhibit of his paintings he created using chicken feet as brushes.

- Warhol made over 300 underground films. *Sleep*, the first, simply showcased a man asleep for six hours.

- In 2006, billionaire collector Eli Broad paid $11.8 million for Andy Warhol's small painting of a can of Campbell's soup.

- The film *I Shot Andy Warhol* was inspired by the SCUM Manifesto, the anti-men rhetoric published by Valerie Solanas in the 1960s. It was originally planned as a documentary, but the filmmakers could not find much footage of Solanas or anyone to speak about her.

Water

🌢 The average person consumes 16,000 gallons of water in a lifetime.

🌢 50% of the world's population does not have an adequate supply of fresh water.

🌢 300 different chemicals can be found in U.S. drinking water.

🌢 Drinking water after a meal reduces the acid in the mouth by 61%.

🌢 At birth, water makes up approximately 80% of an infant's body weight.

🌢 Water intoxication is the over-consumption of water. The excess water dilutes the sodium level in the bloodstream, causing an imbalance of water in the brain, and it can be fatal.

🌢 Pure water has a neutral pH of 7, which is neither acidic nor basic.

🌢 346,000 million gallons of fresh water are used every day in the US.

Wedding

- Brides in ancient Rome carried sheaves of wheat during their weddings as symbols of fertility.

- Brides once carried bouquets of garlic, chives, and rosemary as protection against witches and demons.

- During the Tudor period in England, bridal bouquets were made with marigolds, which were eaten after the ceremony to ensure fertility.

- The tower of St Bride's Church in London inspired the three-tiered cake. A London baker decided to copy the idea as a design for fashionable weddings and it has continued to be as popular today as it was almost three hundred years ago.

- The most expensive wedding was the marriage of Sheik Rashid Bin Saeed Al Maktoum's son to Princess Salama in Dubai in May 1981. Cost? A cool $44 million.

- Traditionally in Sweden, the bride inserts a silver coin from her father and a gold coin from her mother in each shoe to ensure that she will never do without.

Whales

🐋 The brain of a sperm whale can weigh up to 20 lbs making it the largest and heaviest brain on the planet.

🐋 A humpback whale can consume up to a ton of food every day.

🐋 The voice of the blue whale, one of the deepest voices on the planet, is so powerful that it can travel up to 100 miles underwater. The whales sing at frequencies between 10 and 40 Hz, and infrasound less than 20 Hz cannot be heard by humans.

🐋 Scientists have discovered that each whale population has its own "language" which is understood only by those individuals in the population.

🐋 Spermaceti oil, made from the sperm whale, was used as transmission oil in the Rolls Royce.

🐋 A blue whale's tongue weighs more than a whole elephant, and is large enough for fifty people to stand on it.

🐋 In Oklahoma, it is against the law to hunt whales...an odd law as the state is landlocked.

White House

🍂 John Adams was the first president to live in the White House in 1800. During his term, he added a vegetable garden.

🍂 In 1926, the White House had its first electric refrigerator.

🍂 First constructed in 1902 behind the West Wing, the White House tennis court was moved to the west side of the south lawn in 1909 to make room for the expansion of the Executive office space.

🍂 It takes 300 gallons of white paint just to cover the center exterior of the White House, which doesn't include the West and East Wings.

🍂 The White House has 132 rooms, including 16 family-guest rooms, 1 main kitchen, 1 diet kitchen, 1 family kitchen, and 35 bathrooms.

Wine

◦ Foot treading of grapes is still a common procedure in producing small quantities of some of the world's best port wines.

◦ Swirling the glass invites oxygen into the glass, which releases the aromas.

◦ The region of Beaujolais is 34 miles long from north to south and 7 to 9 miles wide. All the grapes in the Beaujolais region must be picked by hand. These are the only vineyards, along with Champagne, where hand harvesting is mandatory.

◦ There are more than 10,000 varieties of grapes grown around the world. It takes an average of four years before newly planted grape vines are harvested for the production of wine.

◦ France produces the largest number of wine cases—averaging 550 *million* each year.

Wonder, Stevie

He was born Steveland Morris and went blind soon after his birth due to a hospital error. By the time he was eight, Stevie was already playing the harmonica, piano and drums.

Stevie Wonder earned his first number-one hit with the song "Fingertips." Both the studio and live versions of the song featured drumming by a future star known as Marvin Gaye.

Peter Frampton, Kim Wilde and Human Nature have covered his hit song "Signed, Sealed, and Delivered."

Wonder is a devoted humanitarian who has contributed to AIDS awareness, anti-apartheid efforts, crusades against drunk driving and drug abuse, and fund raising for the blind and the homeless.

He has earned ten U.S. number-one hits on the pop charts, 20 U.S. R&B number one hits, and album sales totalling more than 150 million units. He was inducted into the Rock & Roll Hall of Fame in 1989.

Aisha Morris, his daughter, inspired the hit single "Isn't She Lovely."

Wonder Woman

- Wonder Woman's real name is Diana Themyscira.

- Her powers include super strength, flight, and the ability to make invisible cars at will. Her weapons of choice are the lasso of truth, unbreakable silver bracelets, and a razor-sharp golden tiara.

- Wonder Woman is 5 ft 11 in and weighs 140 lbs.

- Her silver bracelets are made from a magically indestructible metal in Amazonium.

- The first issue of Gloria Steinham's *Ms.* magazine featured Wonder Woman on the cover. The issue featured an article celebrating the feminist nature of the world's most famous female superhero.

- Lynda Carter had only $25 remaining in her bank account when she received the news that she was cast as Wonder Woman. She beat out 2,000 other actresses for the coveted role.

The X-Factor

🐦 Similar to *American Idol, The X-Factor* is a British television music competition contested by aspiring pop singers drawn from public auditions.

🐦 In the four years up to 2007, more than 375,000 people applied for *The X Factor*—enough harmonies to fill Wembley stadium...over four times.

🐦 The most popular audition song choices for females include "Summertime," "Somewhere Over the Rainbow," "Hero," and "How Do I Live Without You."

🐦 The most popular audition song choices for males are "Ain't No Sunshine," "You Give Me Something, Yesterday," and "I Believe I Can Fly."

🐦 Chanteuse Leona Lewis went from being a pizza waitress to a 2007 *X-Factor* winner to global superstar.

The X-Files

🖎 *The X-Files* is a television series, created by Chris Carter, which first aired in 1993 and ended in 2002. It won numerous accolades including the Peabody, Golden Globe, and Emmy Award.

🖎 William B. Davis, the actor who plays the Cigarette Smoking Man, is also a spokesman for the Canadian Cancer Society. He smoked herbal cigarettes during his scenes.

🖎 The show had no shortage of guest appearances. Jack Black and Giovanni Ribisi shared an episode in season three while Luke Wilson was in season five.

🖎 The episode "Piper Maru" was named after Gillian Anderson's daughter.

🖎 One of Mulder's "connections in Congress"—Senator Matheson—was named after classic sci-fi horror writer named Richard Matheson.

X

Xylophone

- The xylophone was first used in Southeast Asia in the 14th century.

- A xylophone was first used in an orchestral work, in *Danse Macabre* (1874) by French composer Camille Saint-Saens.

- A glockenspiel, a musical instrument similar to the xylophone, has a series of metal bars and is played with two hammers.

- Total recall! In 2009, The Land of Nod recalled its Rolling Toy Xylophones after receiving numerous reports about pieces of the toy breaking off. The pegs on the xylophone could break off and posed choking hazards to children. About 500 toys were included in the recall.

- In July 2004 in Nottingham, UK, a beloved street performer named "Xylophone Man" passed away from a heart attack. After more than a decade on the streets, Xylophone Man was instantly recognizable to a wide range of the public. Although he reportedly wasn't very good at the xylophone, he certainly made up for it in heart.

X

Yellow

❧ During the Elizabethan Era, English Law dictated who could wear the color yellow since both color and material used during this era were extremely important.

❧ Leonardo da Vinci wrote that the color yellow represented earth.

❧ "High yellow" was a term for very light-skinned, multiracial people who also had African ancestry, but the term is rarely used today.

❧ Jaundice is the yellow discoloration of the skin caused by excessive amounts of bilirubin (the product of hemoglobin breakdown) in the blood.

❧ "Mellow Yellow," was the hit song by Donovan. Though many speculated that the song was about smoking banana skins, this was just an urban myth. It was actually Country Joe McDonald who, in 1966, started the rumor that one could get high from smoking dried banana skins.

Y

Yo-yos

❧ The yo-yos today are based on a hunting aid created by Filipino tribe people. The orb was used to stun and disorient while the twine came in handy to trip the animals. An American businessman saw the novelty and turned the weapon into a toy in the 1920s.

❧ The world's largest yo-yo resides in the National Yo-Yo Museum in Chico, CA. Named "Big Yo," the 256-pound yo-yo is made of California sugar pine, Baltic birch from the former USSR, and hardrock maple.

❧ Various yo-yo tricks include "Walk the Dog," "Hop the Fence," "Man on a Flying Trapeze," "Rock the Cradle," and "Skin the Cat."

❧ The World Yo-Yo Contest was first started in 1932 in London, England. As of 2006, 19 countries participated in the World Yo-Yo Contest and 700 people were in attendance.

❧ The World Yo-Yo Contest also acts as the host for the World Spin Top Contest and the World Throw Dough Championships every year.

Y

Yodel

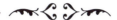

- A yodel is a type of wordless singing usually associated with the Swiss, but is practiced as much in the Alps as it is in the mountains of Kentucky.

- The best environments for Alpine-style yodeling have an echo and include lakes, rocky gorges, long hallways, rocky shorelines sporting canoes, and of course, the best environment of all, a mountain range.

- Yodels require breaks between high and low notes and it's the epiglottis, a human physiological feature, which allows for emphasizing the breaks.

- In Persian and Azeri classical music, singers employ a yodeling technique called *tahrir*, which oscillates on neighboring tones.

- On October 8, 2002, 937 yodelers held a melody for a minute at the Ravensburger Amusement Park near the German town of Meckenbeuren. They set the world record for the largest simultaneous yodel.

Y

Yogurt

 ❧ Americans consume more than 300,000 tons of yogurt each year.

 ❧ Fruit was first added to commercially-produced yogurt in the U.S. by Dannon Yogurt.

 ❧ It takes about 1 pound of whole milk to make 1 pound of yogurt.

 ❧ In Armenia, yogurt is called *matzoon* and in Egypt, it's called *leben raib*.

 ❧ Preliminary studies show increasing one's dietary intake of low fat, calcium-rich dairy products such as yogurt may reduce the risk of colon cancer.

Y

Zebra

❧ Zebras, like horses and wild asses, are equids—long-legged animals that can move swiftly for their large size and have teeth designed for grinding and cropping grass.

❧ Zebras communicate by positioning their ears and tails.

❧ The long-legged Grevy's zebra is the biggest of the wild equids. Named after a 19-century French president who received one as a present, Grevy's zebras can be found in Northern Kenya.

❧ The Romans used to call Grevy's zebras "hippotigris" and used them in circus exhibitions to pull two-wheeled carts.

❧ Zebras are black with white stripes…not vice versa.

❧ The black and white stripes form a type of camouflage known as "disruptive coloration," which breaks up the outline of the body. Like fingerprints, the pattern is unique for every zebra.

❧ The zebra's shiny coat dissipates over 70% of incoming heat.

Z

Zedong, Mao

- "An army without culture is a dull-witted army, and a dull-witted army cannot defeat the enemy."

- On September 9, 1976, Mao died at the age of 82 and was embalmed. His corpse was laid in a sarcophagus on permanent public display in a mausoleum in Tiananmen Square in Beijing. Each night when the museum is closed, the sarcophagus is lowered into an earthquake-proof chamber below the square.

- The Chairman was married four times and was convinced that having sex with virgins helped "to restore and reinvigorate a man's health and vigor."

- Mao was responsible for 14 to 20 million deaths from starvation during the "Great Leap Forward" with tens of thousands killed and millions of lives ruined during the "Cultural Revolution."

- Mao Zedong loved to swim. In his youth, he promoted swimming as a way of empowering the bodies of Chinese citizens, and one of his earliest poems embraced the beating of a wake through the waves. He swam avidly throughout his entire life.

- The book *Mao: the Unknown Story* alleged that Mao was aware of the vast suffering and deaths from the "Great Leap Forward" but was dismissive of it, instead blaming bad weather or other officials for the famine.

Zipper

- The initials YKK commonly seen on most zippers stands for "Yoshida Kogyo Kabushibibaisha," the world's largest zipper manufacturer.

- Whitcomb L. Judson, a mechanical engineer from Chicago, invented a number of labor-efficient items, including the zipper.

- It was B.F. Goodrich who coined the term zipper when he placed a large order for rubber galoshes he was manufacturing. He liked the "z-z-zip" sound they made and coined the name.

- Initially, clothing with zippers was viewed as inappropriate for women because clothing could be removed so quickly. For this reason, zippers were found mostly in men's and children's apparel for years.

- Zippers were originally used primarily for boots and tobacco pouches. Two decades later, the fashion industry introduced them for children's clothes. You can imagine how excited men were when they began placing them on their pants!

Z

Zombies

◆ The bubonic plague not only wiped out half of Europe at one time, it also spawned many stories of zombies. Tales of the recently deceased and walking dead began to appear across the continent. Some of the symptoms of the bubonic plague—including passing out, falling into a brief comatose state, and internal bleeding—likely contributed to the notion of zombies.

◆ In the early 19th century, electrophysiologists thought that the right dosage of electricity charged to the brain could bring a corpse back to life.

◆ Rob Zombie, the accomplished musician and front man of the band White Zombie (named after the film), has directed several horror films including *House of 1000 Corpses* and *Devil's Rejects*. His remake of *Halloween* earned $78 million at the box office. Rob is certainly more human than human in terms of achievements.

◆ With a budget of $500,000, Michael Jackson's "Thriller" (1983) had the highest budget for a music video at the time. In 2006, Guinness World Records awarded it the "most successful music video," having sold over 9 million units.

◆ Zombie flick *Resident Evil* (2002) starring Milla Jovovich was originally titled *Resident Evil: Ground Zero*. They dropped the subtitle after the September 11th attacks on New York City.

Z

Bibliography

Ashbaugh, David, R. *Ridgeology: Journal of Forensic Identification Vol. 41. Canada.* Royal Canadian Mounted Police. 1989.

Barnham, Andrea. *The Pendant's Revolt: Why Most Things You Think Are Right Are Wrong.* London. Michael O'Mara Books Limited. 2005.

Bombaugh, C. C. *Oddities and Curiosities of Words and Literature.* New York. Dover Publications, Inc. 1961.

Botham, Noel. *The Ultimate Book of Useless Information.* London. John Blake Publishing. 2003.

Carr, Carolyn Kinder. *Americans: Paintings and Photographs from the National Portrait Gallery, Washington DC.* New York. Watson-Guptill Publications. 2002.

Clairborne, Craig. *The New York Times Food Encyclopedia.* New York. Random House. 1994.

Cummins, Harold. "Ancient finger prints in clay," *The Scientific Monthly, vol. 52:* 389–402.

Evans, Ivor H. *Brewer's Dictionary of Phrase & Fable.* New York. Harper & Row. 1981.

Feldman, David. *How Do Astronauts Scratch an Itch?* New York. G.P. Putnam's Sons. 1996.

Glenday, Craig, ed. *Guinness World Records 2009*. London. Guinness World Records Limited. 2008.

Homer, Trevor. T*he Book of Origins: The First of Everything from Art to Zoos*. London. Portrait. 2006.

Koehn, Nancy F. "Henry Heinz and Brand Creation in the Late Nineteenth Century: Making Markets for Processed Food." *The Business History Review, Vol. 73*. Autumn 1999: 349–393.

Lennox, Doug. *Now You Know: The Book of Answers*. Toronto. Dundurn Press. 2003.

Levy, Ariel. *Female Chauvinist Pigs: Women and the Rise of Raunch Culture,* New York. Free Press. 2006.

Lloyd, John, and Mitchison, John. *The Book of General Ignorance*. London. Faber and Faber. 2006.

Mooney, Julie. *Ripley's Believe it or Not: Encyclopedia of the bizarre, amazing, strange, inexplicable, Weird, and All True!*. New York. Black Dog & Levanthal Publishers, Inc. 2002.

The New York Times. *New York Times Guide to Essential Knowledge: A Desk Reference for the Curious Mind*. New York. St. Martin's Press. 2004.

Quackenbos, George Payn. *A Natural Philosophy: Embracing the Most Recent Discoveries in the Various Branches of Physics, and Exhibiting the Application of Scientific Principles in Every-Day Life*. Boston. Adamant Media Corporation. 2005.

Ridpath, Ian, ed. *The Illustrated Encyclopedia of the Universe.* New York. Watson-Guptill Publications. 2001.

Rubenzer, Steven J. and Faschingbauer, Thomas R. *Personality, Character, and Leadership in the White House: Psychologists Assess the Presidents.* Dulles. Potomac Books, Inc. 2004.

Schott, Ben. *Schott's Miscellany: 2008.* New York. Bloomsbury. 2007.

Schott, Ben. *Schott's Original Miscellany.* New York. Bloomsbury. 2003.

Sears, George Washington. *Woodcraft and Camping.* New York. Dover Publications, Inc. 1963.

Stefaniuk, Walter. *501 Things You Really Should Know.* Toronto. West-End Books. 2005.

Stein, Melissa, ed. *The Wit and Wisdom of Women.* Philadelphia. Running Press. 1993.

Stevenson, Burton. *The Home Book of Quotations: Classical and Modern, 10th ed.* New York. Dodd, Mead & Company. 1967.

Tansey, Geoff and D'Silva, Joyce. *The Meat Business: Devouring a Hungry Planet.* Basingstoke. Palgrave Macmillan. 1999.

Thieret, John W., et al. *National Audubon Society Field Guide to North American Wildflowers, Eastern Region, Rev. Ed.* New York. Alfred A Knopf. 2001.

Turnball, Stephen and Noon, Steve. *The Great Wall of China 221 BC–AD 1644.* New York. Osprey Publishing. 2007.

Wallechinsky, David, et al. *The Book of Lists: The Original Compendium of Curious Information: The Canadian Edition.* Toronto, Ont. Alfred A. Knopf Canada. 2005.

Zimmerman, Michael E., et al. *Environmental Philosophy: From Animal Rights to Deep Ecology.* Englecliffs. Prentice-Hall. 1993.